LETTERS

LETTERS

Marjorie Pay Hinckley

DESERET BOOK

SALT LAKE CITY, UTAH

The publisher expresses thanks to the family of Marjorie Pay Hinckley for graciously sharing these letters to benefit the Missionary Book of Mormon Fund.

Library of Congress Cataloging-in-Publication Data

Hinckley, Marjorie Pay.
  [Correspondence. Selections]
  Letters / Marjorie Pay Hinckley.
      p.   cm.
  ISBN 1-59038-387-7 (hardcover : alk. paper)
  1. Hinckley, Marjorie Pay—Correspondence.   2. Mormons—Biography.
3. Mormons—Religious life.   I. Title.
  BX8695.H57A4 2004
  289.3'092—dc22

                                                              2004017698

Printed in the United States of America   72076
Publishers Printing, Salt Lake City, UT

10 9   8   7   6   5   4   3   2

Contents

Introduction

July 20, 2004
Salt Lake City, Utah

Dear Reader,

It is a bright summer morning in the Valley of the Great Salt Lake as we write this letter. There are a few wispy clouds in a blue sky, and the mountains still have just a bit of snow. We have been reading some of our mother's letters and having a wonderful time.

Our parents belong to what may be the last generation of letter writers. For them, letters were the primary means of communication with family members separated by distance. Telegrams and long-distance telephone calls were expensive and used only for emergencies or very special occasions. There was no e-mail or instant messaging. So writing letters was part of life's routine. When family members lived out of town, letters traveled back and forth and kept them connected. Even when traveling on vacation, people sent letters and postcards as a link to those left behind.

In the spectrum of communication, a letter falls somewhere between a conversation and a journal entry. Conversations are spontaneous and real, but they are subject to the vagaries of memory, and our memories seem to be getting less reliable every year. Journals are a gift to future generations, but they are often stilted, self-conscious, and wooden. Although journal entries can be enlightening and deeply personal, they are written not to an individual but to some ethereal "Dear Diary" or to posterity as a whole.

Ah, but a letter . . . a letter is written to a real person, flesh and blood. Both the writer and the recipient are in the middle of life, not off in some theoretical laboratory. Letters always have context. They exist within the political and social times. Personal and public events provide context, and letters always live in the context of relationships. Best of all, letters are there to be read again, years later, word for word as they were written. That is, if the recipient is smart enough to save them!

Mother wrote letters to her parents, to her siblings, to our father, to each of us, and to each of our children. She sometimes wrote group letters, but more often, she wrote to us one at a time, during the times we individually lived away from Salt Lake City. Of all of the things that she left behind when she passed away at the age of ninety-two, we treasure nothing more than her letters and postcards. Sadly enough, most of us failed to keep these treasures. Kathy, alone, seems to have been the most consistent keeper of Mother's letters, as you will notice in the pages of this little book. We are so grateful to her. Are oldest children *always* the most responsible about *everything*?

Addressed to Kathy or not, we love reading and rereading Mother's letters. We hear her voice; she returns to our circle and helps us remember earlier times. We read her questions and remember the answers we might have given. We see in our memory the familiar surroundings of long-gone days. In the touch of the paper and the tidy, small handwriting we are tangibly connected again.

We cannot think of a way that she could have better passed on her faith in us and in the gospel. Never preachy or critical, her values and good advice were woven together with genuine love. Her letters were uniformly affirming, nourishing, reassuring, encouraging, lighthearted, and fortifying. We always felt that she found great pleasure in us, even though we caused her no end of irritation and hard work. Her excitement about life, people, and this amazing world fairly leapt off the pages and into our hearts. Her news bulletins about members of the family bound us to one another when we were too busy to stay in constant touch ourselves. Through her letters, we also came to understand more fully her love and affection for our father as well as her complete and wholehearted devotion to the Kingdom. Although her behavior and conversations always reflected these things, they seem to be so clearly articulated in her letters. In fact, letters provide just enough distance that we can sometimes say the sweet things that we might be a bit too timid to say face-to-face.

Frankly, we feel reluctant to publish these letters, wondering how an unrelated reader could possibly find them interesting. However, on reflection, we know that we find it a rare treat to read family letters of others. We are always curious to know what it might be like to live in someone else's family. So perhaps you might like to know what our mother said to us, to our father, to her parents, or to her siblings when no one else was listening. Perhaps you wonder about the dailyness of someone else's life—

the behind-closed-doors thoughts and tasks that you know about your own family but can only guess about others.

We have also resisted the publication of these letters for fear it may appear that we are exploiting Mother's life for financial gain. We have consented only with the understanding that all royalties will go to the Missionary Book of Mormon Fund. She would have welcomed the opportunity to further the distribution of that sacred volume, which she constantly read and from which she frequently quoted.

And so, we offer this sampling of Mother's letters. They appear essentially as she wrote them, although names of people other than family members have been omitted, and some standardizing of spelling and punctuation has been done. We hope that you will see them as a celebration of the power of the ordinary. We hope that as you peek into the Monday, Tuesday, and Wednesday-ness of her life, you will see with new eyes the value of your own. And, most of all, we hope that your family will decide to write and save more letters.

Having a wonderful time. We only wish you were here, Mother!

Sincerely,

The Children of Marjorie Pay Hinckley

Kathleen Barnes Walker, Richard Hinckley, Virginia Pearce,
Clark Hinckley, Jane Dudley

Letters from
a Young Wife
and Mother

*T*he letters in this first section were written in 1945, which was an unusual year for the Hinckley family. World War II was still raging, and Gordon had left employment with the Church and was working with the Denver & Rio Grande Railroad as part of the war effort. He arrived in Denver in October 1944, but wartime housing shortages made it difficult to find a place suitable to accommodate his growing family. Despite his relentless searching, he was unable to secure a home to rent until January 1945, at which time Marjorie and the children joined him.

It was Marjorie's first time living away from her family, and her letters home to her parents and younger siblings (she was the oldest child) reflect both her homesickness and her continued interest in their lives. She had two small children and was expecting a third, so we get an intimate picture of a mother's concerns. Beyond that, the letters offer an interesting view of everyday life in America during wartime.

Marjorie Hinckley with her children Dick and Kathy

Marjorie wrote this letter, expressing her frustration with an uncooperative furnace, just before joining her husband in Denver. There were no gas lines running out to East Mill Creek, so a coal furnace was the only option. The stoker was an automatic mechanism to feed the furnace so the coal did not have to be shoveled. Gordon returned to Salt Lake City the following weekend, fixed the furnace, and accompanied Marjorie and the children back to Denver on the train.

Salt Lake City, Utah
January 9, 1945

Dearest!

This is Tuesday morning—almost time for the mailman, so I'll take a few minutes to tell you my troubles.

For two days the stoker has only gone on when the pin was pushed. I just went down and pushed the pin, as the fire was getting very low. The belt went forward for about half a round jerkily, as if it were caught, and then the whole thing stopped as dead as if the power had been turned off. I can move the belt freely by hand, but can't get a spark of life anywhere. I have promised the house to the renters on the 15th and am very much upset about this stoker business. Unless we can get it on some kind of dependable basis I wonder if these people will want to rent the place if the furnace must be hand fed, as that was a feature they were most concerned about. Frankly, I've about given up on this stoker, but perhaps I shouldn't feel so, as it may be something very minor which I do not understand. Ignorance is *not* bliss in this case.

Kathie is much better today—fever is down, but she still has too much tightness on her chest to suit me, although I think we will have her pretty much on top by the end of the week.

At any rate, if we are to come this weekend it would be much better if you could come home—particularly to see about the stoker. Am looking forward with great pleasure toward living with a man in a house with a gas furnace. Happy day!

Cheerful epistle for you to start your day's work on, but all is well that ends well and when we are again settled and together it will be a very nice world. Guess you are more essential in my life than I had guessed. Just don't seem to be able to get along without you. Love you like everything.

Marge

This letter was written the first week after Marjorie arrived in Denver with her two children, Kathie, age 5, and Dick, age 3.

January 20, 1945

Dear Family,

Evelyn's card arrived yesterday and was most welcome, as it was the first word from home. The kids haven't given home a single thought since they left until yesterday morning (before the card arrived). Kathie said, "I wish Grandma or some of those kids would ever write us a letter," so she was happy to get the card, and the letter forwarded from Helen was very choice, too.

Dickie has been under the weather ever since we arrived. Tuesday and Wednesday he had the worst croup of his young career. The doctor here says croup is a sort of spasm, a miserable but not serious affliction, but when his fever got up to 104½ the doctor sent a baby specialist out to the house. Of course, by the time the doctor arrived Dickie's fever was down and he was singing "Don't Fence Me In." The doctor said he had a streptococcus throat infection (which is a fancy name for old-fashioned sore throat) along with the croup. We have been giving him sulfa and he is better now. He played around the house all day yesterday, but he seems a little drowsy and sick to his stomach today, as a result of the sulfa. But I am not worried about him, as his temperature has been normal for two days.

Kathie feels better and looks better than she has for weeks. I think it was a good deal to have that bothersome tooth out.

This is a nice neighborhood, made up largely of young couples with small children. There are two nice little girls across the street just Kathie's age and they will all go to school together, so it will work out very well, as the school is 14 blocks away and there is no school bus to take them at noon. The mothers on the street take turns taking them at noon on the public bus and then the school bus brings them home. We are going to try to get to town next week to get her some school dresses, and is she ever thrilled!

I think I will do without my dinner set until we have the car here to bring them from the express company to the house, as they charge $3 for a trip out here. Gordon says in order to find 1195 So. Cook you go to the center of town and then go east, halfway to Kansas City and there you are. By the way, it will only cost $1.15 to phone Helen from here, so I am going to splurge one of these first days. It only costs 75 cents for 3 minutes at night to S.L.C. so I'll give you a buzz sometime too.

The neighbors are very nice. There is one across the street about my age who is from the South. Her name is Kathleen, but they call her Kay so it's not as confusing as it might be. When she heard that Dickie has the croup she was over here at 9:15 in the morning with a steam inhalator, lemons, mustard, and all the fixings. Although everyone seems very nice they somehow seem different from folks at home. They are all from some other town—no relatives, no roots—and yet in friendliness and kindliness have it over on most of us.

I didn't think any place outside the garden of Eden could be this clean. Haven't swept the bathroom floor since I got here. There's just nothing to sweep up. As a matter of fact, haven't swept the kitchen for 3 days—just run the cedar mop over it. This is certainly the life. In fact it is too easy. I would do better if there were a little to do, but as soon as I can get to town for a few things I will be able to occupy my time getting ready for the stork. And, of course, when the iron arrives I will be able to rig up a couple of days work. Happy thought.

I am going downstairs now and try out the fancy washer and mangle on some bedding. Tomorrow being Saturday I think I shall try to go to Gaylords, which is the Sugarhouse for this district, while Gordon stays home with Dickie, so if you don't hear from me for some time you'd better notify the lost and found department. I'm apt to end up in Kansas City or Colorado Springs. I have been poring over a map of the streetcar and bus lines, and it is nothing short of bewildering.

All my love,

Marjorie

Her third child would arrive within two weeks, so Marjorie's first foray out into the city was to meet her new obstetrician. Gasoline was severely rationed due to the war, and driving was held to an absolute minimum. Driving speed was also restricted to 35 m.p.h. to preserve fuel. At any rate, the Hinckleys would not bring their car to Denver until sometime in March, so they relied exclusively on public transportation during the winter of 1945. The "Assistant Superintendent of Mail, Baggage, and Express" she refers to in this letter is her husband.

Denver, Colorado
January 26, 1945
Friday morning

Dear Family,

The time certainly is going by. This is getting near the end of the second week. The first three days lasted for about six weeks apiece, but this week has been a little better. Of all the mumps and measles I have had, homesickness is the worst. Wow! If you've never had it, you don't know what you've missed. When the doctor asked me if I had had any of the major diseases, I told him "yes," that I was just recuperating from one of the worst. And I didn't get the least bit of sympathy around here. I'd just get my mind off it and Gordon would say, "So you're homesick, are you?" and then he would shake with laughter while I ran for a handkerchief to blow. He had had his turn. However, I'm doing much better now. I can listen to the radio announcer say "This is K.V.O.D. *Denver*," without even batting an eye.

We surely had a time on Wednesday when we went to town. I was lost all the way in and all the way back. I had a map with the bus route on it, but by the time I could see a street sign and look it up on the map we'd be three miles past it. You see, the trouble is that you have to transfer at one of three places in order to get into town. And besides that there was a fierce blizzard blowing that day. There were several school children on the bus going to the Washington Park School, so I figured I could at least get myself located when they got off at the school. But according to my map they got off at the wrong corner and walked the wrong direction. By the time I decided I was hopeless and asked the motorman where I should get off, we had turned around and were a third of the way back home, but I didn't know it. I had intended to do a little shopping in town, but as soon as I got the Metropolitan Building, where the doctor was, spotted, I didn't dare let it out of my sight. So I just went in one little crockery store and got some Pyrex while Kathie stood at the door with her eyes glued on the Metropolitan Building. Then we went to the doctor's and straight home. That is, as straight as you can go in this crooked town. There was a man on the bus coming home with his collar on backwards, and since the Catholic School is right across the street from us, we just followed him.

I feel all right about the doctor here. He was very nice and gave me the most thorough examination I have ever had. He is in his late forties, I imagine—maybe 50—has a good-sized family of his own, and should know what it's all about. I go to St. Luke's hospital, which is near the center of town. There are dozens of hospitals in this town, according to this map, but I don't believe everything this map says anymore. St. Luke's is one of the oldest, but is supposed to be one of the largest and best equipped. I just hope it doesn't have dark halls with statues in the corners, and bats in the beams.

This is a peculiar town. There was a lady crossing the intersection just ahead of us when we got off the bus in town. She was carrying a large, awkward bundle. Another lady rushed up to see if she could help her with the package. The first lady said, "I'll bet you could never guess in a million years what's in this package. I tried all morning to get a cab, but couldn't," and away the two ladies go up the street chattering away as if they were old friends. A few minutes later when we were standing in front of the crockery store a man came dashing by, then suddenly swung around and started kidding the children a bit. Told me about his oldest daughter who was now married and had a child of her own—about his son in the army—how he felt about life in general, then said, "Well, good-day," tipped his hat and rushed on up the street. They certainly are an amusing crowd.

I can't buy any infant shirts here. Each morning I go right down the list of department stores in the yellow pages, but all they say is, "Sorry, we're right out." But I suppose one of these mornings someone will say, "Why, yes, we just got some in today," and then the problem will be to get the Assistant Superintendent of Mail, Baggage, and Express to pick them up. But he is really improving. He is so afraid something drastic will happen if I go shopping around in this busy city. He makes a stop in Grant's Department Store nearly every evening. Last night he brought some drinking glasses and a pair of pepper and salts on which he had bargained the clerk down from 39 cents to 25 cents because they were both pepper shakers.

I don't dare go to church until we get the car, because it involves so much walking and waiting around for buses, and it is almost impossible to get a taxi in this town, unless it is an emergency. Don't believe there are any L.D.S.'ers on our street but apparently there are several in this vicinity, according to the block teachers who called the other evening.

Don't know which I am looking forward to the most—the baby or your visit. We will send the empty suitcases over before long and you can bring them back full when you come. Whatever else we need we will put in the back seat of the car when it comes. The dishes are still a question. If the war should end this summer perhaps we'll be home before we need them.

By the way, if we don't get new gas stamps until the end of March I don't know what it would profit us to bring the car over before then, as there were only two 14's and that one "C" ticket left and we owed you all of those for the trips you made to 3703. Please advise on this.

If nothing drastic happens by the 18th perhaps you should plan to leave by then anyway. The lady across the street has offered to take care of Kathie and Dickie until you get here if necessary, but it would be much better, of course, if you could already be here, as no telling how long it will take to get a reservation.

Well, the paper has run out and last night's company dishes are still in the sink, so will sign off for now.

Love and kisses,

Marjorie

Transportation during the war continued to be one of the overriding facts of daily life. Marjorie realized it would be a sacrifice for her mother to come and help care for the new baby because she would be leaving four younger children at home. Marjorie's sister Helen was on a mission in Chicago. The baby was born on February 8, the day after this letter was written.

February 7, 1945

Dear Mamma and Papa
and all my little sisters,

I am enclosing a claim check. The first one to present this at the Baggage Room of the D. & R. G. W. S. L. C. Ut. will receive Evelyn's empty suitcase all wrapped in paper. There is a D. & R. G. bus which goes down Main Street every little while, so if you don't have the car in town perhaps Daddy could take a bus ride down there after work.

This suitcase is for Mother to use to bring her personals to Denver. As for the rest of our things, could you put the baby things—diapers, night-gowns, receiving blankets, hot pad, my pinafore, blue flowered housedress, green dress with yellow buttons, and my best brown dress—in a strong cardboard box and have it expressed. It shouldn't weigh too much, being all dry goods, and this way will be delivered right to the house. This is quite an advantage, because it is such a problem to get things to and from the R. R.

station on these crowded Denver buses—which is the reason we only sent one suitcase. The express company should pick this box up at the house, which will save you taking it to town to be mailed.

Inside the suitcase you will find a windshield wiper for the car, which G. has written Douglas about.

Also look in that blue case which fits inside the trunk and see if there is anything which could come in the express box or in your suitcase. I am particularly interested in getting our cancelled checks for October, November, and December, which might be in that blue box. Anything else we need will have to wait until the car comes and we can then put the fruit, books, scooters, tricycle, etc. in the backseat.

We are still undecided about how to get the car here. If Daddy could drive it over it would be fine, as we could then load it with a lot of our belongings, which we would feel hesitant to do if some stranger were bringing it over. However, I doubt that the car could average much better than 35 or 40 miles an hour, particularly coming over those high passes in the middle of the winter. This would make it a slow, long trip and if I should go to the hospital before you leave we would want you to come faster than the old jalopy could make it.

By the way (I'm almost afraid to mention this for fear you might take me up on it) would you like me to inquire around and see if we could get someone here to come and help, so you would not have to come over? I have made no attempt to see if we could get anyone, but if you would like me to I will see what the prospects are. As the time approaches for you to leave I know it presents many problems at home, such as the laundry, etc.—especially when you have to be away for such a long time. Maybe you would rather postpone your trip to Denver until it is time for Helen to come home (I don't hope). However, I know it will be hard for you to leave the family in the winter, so let me know how things are shaping up and if you would like me to see what I can do here. I will at least try, although I don't know what luck I would have.

Well, it's late at night and everyone in the house is asleep and I'm getting the fever, too, so will say goodnight. After all, this letter will keep you out of mischief for a few days.

Had a perfectly wonderful card from Evelyn today and a perfectly super letter from Mother yesterday. Not doing so bad this week.

Love to you all,

Marjorie

XXOOXXOO

Marjorie's mother went to Denver and stayed for several weeks after the baby's birth. She had just returned home when this letter was written.

Denver, Colorado
March 9, 1945

Dear Folksies, including Helen,

Just received Mother's letter reporting her safe return. Don't know whether to feel like a heel for keeping you away from the family for so long or like a good kid for making them appreciate you so much. We heard that the train was late getting into S.L. and I was so afraid Daddy wouldn't be able to be there. Think it is swell-er-ee that Dorene and Joanne stayed home. That must have been quite a homecoming with all the signs! Maybe you should come back and visit me again—it sounds so much fun to go home. If you are feeling bad about leaving the dishes and ironing I'll be glad to save them for you. I'm surprised that I haven't been more homesick since you left. Felt pretty low Monday afternoon, but since then haven't been nearly as homesick as I was before you came—and I might add, before the baby came. She keeps my mind off all the morbid things of life during war time.

Dickie is ever so much better. His cough is gone. His gland is still swollen and his temperature hangs between normal and 99½—100. I talked to Dr. B. yesterday. He said he would probably have a little temp. as long as the gland was swollen and he wants me to keep him quiet until that is under control. Keeping him quiet is no small job, as he feels so well and is eating wonderfully. You know those P.J.'s he cut the bottoms off? Well last night he cut a round hole in each knee, so today I put his Levis on. Kathie went to school Monday, but has been home ever since with sniffles and a slight fever. Isn't it disgusting, to say the least? However, she doesn't feel sick and I don't keep her down.

It was surely wonderful to get a copy of Helen's letter this week. I hope you'll keep sending me a carbon even though Mother isn't here. I'll send you copies of my letters home, too, and then we can all keep up on the news. You sounded so natural on the phone. It was so fun but so short. Dickie was sick that night or he would have said his 2 cents worth too, but we will call you again sometime. Kathie got such a thrill out of it. She just about jumped out of her skin while we were waiting for the operator to get the call through.

I do hope Daddy is beginning to feel better. Maybe he will feel better now Mother is home to make him a batch of bread. Ain't fun, is it, Daddy—I mean for one to be in Denver and one in S. L. Just wanted you to know how it felt so you would appreciate why I came here. Now if you and Mother would like to come over together you can see the sights and really enjoy the trip. It grieves me to think that Mother was here for a whole month and didn't see anything, but with Dickie sick and no car, it was just an impossible situation.

I wish you kids—namely, my younger sisters, would send me your reactions to the names we are considering for Madame X. I am beginning to favor "Margo," but, as Gordon says, don't know as how well it would wear. Other probables:

Janet

Virginia

Frances

Please send me your reactions.

Well, I must get busy again. It surely is tough to have to work for a living since Mother went home.

Love to all of you, from all *five* of us. I'm not so very homesick, but I'm beginning to count the months until May.

XO

Marjorie

Rheumatic fever is an inflammatory disease that may develop after an infection with strep-tococcus bacteria and is responsible for many cases of damaged heart valves. Though he had not yet been diagnosed, Dick's heart murmur may have been the first indication that he was suffering from that illness.

Denver, Colorado
March 26, 1945

Dear Family,

Here 'tis a week and a day since I last wrote. I'm not doing so well and could take my hat off to Helen as a correspondent. She is really on the beam when it comes to getting the mail out on time and regularly. I'm afraid the pillow case would have been damp again if her letter hadn't arrived right on time last Wednesday. But then it wasn't as bad because Mother's letter came the next day and they were both delicious.

Grant Hinckley spent a couple of days here the first part of the week on his way home from Washington, D. C. He is good company and it was something to have an honest-to-goodness relative in the house. That is the worst part of this business—no relatives.

The babe is beginning to fret so I'm afraid this letter will not be up to much, as it is almost time for her 10 p.m. feeding. I don't know where the time goes. Seems like it is time to go to bed just as I begin to get started.

Guess I'm a little slow on the start. We've been to the doctor today and it is quite a job to get all three ready and transported. The babe has had diarrhea for *10* days, so I spend most of my time pinning and unpinning but she certainly is getting cuter every day. The doctor says I must take her off the bottle entirely until she is over the trouble and nurse her exclusively, even if she has to go a little hungry. Dick has a definite murmur in his heart and the doctor wants to take his tonsils out as soon as possible, which may not be very soon, as one practically has to be in a state of emergency in order to get a hospital reservation and he has about 30 other children on the waiting list before Dick. The doctor says he thinks all the trouble from this last sickness suddenly localized in his tonsils as they are very bad and his heart would have a much better chance to mend if he would have them out. I worry about him, but then I guess this is all part of raising a family and after all we have been and are very fortunate.

Kathie is giving a poem on the Sunday School Easter program! She is really thrilled about it. My, how she is changing since starting school. We couldn't find a poem, having no books over here, so we wrote our own. What do you think of our humble efforts:

> *"Some folks think that Easter time*
> *Is just for pretty clothes*
> *And Easter baskets filled with eggs*
> *of colors bright and bold.*
> *But Mother told me differently*
> *It's for another reason*

> *For Jesus rose up from His Tomb*
> *at Happy Easter season.*
> *This gives to me a precious gift*
> *It means that when I die*
> *I'll live again, as Jesus did,*
> *And dwell with Him on High."*

Pretty snazzy, eh? She says it real cute (says her mother). I got her some new white slippers and a flowered chintz dress for Easter and is she crazy about the shoes! Oh my! I also got some new brown shoes and she thinks they are bee-utiful because the heels are higher than I usually wear.

Well, the baby's cries are drowning out the news broadcast. Guess I'll have to quit for now. Her hair is still red and I mean *red*—not reddish. Her eyes are still *blue,* but I'm not counting on that. Her hair sticks up on top like a rooster's comb all the time. She weighs 10 lb. 7 oz., I don't know whether it's just because I'm her mother, but she surely is a cute baby. Her eyelashes are about a mile long already—well, at least ⅛ inch. She loves to be cuddled. It's a good thing I don't have a rocking chair. I'm behind on my work as it is.

All our love,

Marjorie

Despite the move to Denver, Gordon Hinckley was not released from the Sunday School general board, and this letter mentions a visit from several fellow board members from Salt Lake City.

Denver, Colorado
April 25, 1945

Dear Family,

The weather in Colorado is worse than disgusting. It is cold, and it snows and blows and rains every day. Last night when the radio announcer read the weather forecast he said, "Wednesday—Fair and warmer, it says here." And he was right, it only said there, 'cause it's still winter.

Dickie is feeling wonderful. We had one warm day—last Saturday—and he got a beautiful suntan. That is, it is beautiful now. Saturday night and Sunday his face, neck, and ears and arms were as red as fire, but it wasn't very sore. I wish spring would come to stay, so he could get out again. We had two days, through Saturday and Sunday, with everyone feeling right on top, but of course that would never do, so Kathie got a humdinger of a cold come Monday morning. She hasn't been to school yet as she is still hoarse and coughing, but has not felt sick with it. Now if Dickie just doesn't get it from her all will be well. They just started on the second box of vitamins at $3.60 a box and the $2.75 bottle of Cod Liver oil is almost empty. The high cost of fighting the common cold is, well, high to say the least.

Sunday we had the best day since we hit this state. It was Sunday School convention. W. A. didn't come, but they sent N. K. and C. A., who are both about our age and loads of fun. They were here for dinner, back for supper, and in the evening we had the Stake Sunday School Superintendency and wives here and showed some slides of scenic Utah. I don't know whether or not the guests enjoyed it, but I had a wonderful time. Sister P., who is from the 4th Ward in S. L., has been here 19 years and is still so homesick she can't talk about it without crying. One picture showed some sagebrush and she exclaimed, "See there, they don't even have the same weeds in Colorado." We laughed at her until we were sick, but it's really kinda sad. I feel for her.

I repeat, I enjoyed the day immensely. We served ice cream with fresh strawberries and chocolate cake. They all raved about the baby's titian hair and she grinned at everyone who spoke to her. She surely was cute. Oh yes—she laughs out loud now and everyone makes such a fuss over her hair that even her Pa is beginning to think maybe she's got a good thing there. Can't wait for you to see her.

Thursday evening we are having the W's. (strong Lutherans) and the D's. (strong reformed Dutch) here for the evening. Mr. D. studied for the ministry before he contracted T.B. and had to give it up. They have a lot of peculiar ideas about the Mormons. We told them we would show them some slides of scenic Utah, but we can also slip in a few on the temples and maybe straighten them out on a few things. They were shocked to learn that we were married in the temple because of the fantastic stories they have heard of temple ceremonies. These people are from the office.

Must get busy now. Have to wash my hair and the diapers and do some ironing today.

Don't know yet when I'll be coming. Think I'll stay put until the weather gets more settled.

Love to everyone,

Marjorie

President Heber J. Grant died May 14, 1945, just one month after President Franklin D. Roosevelt's death on April 12, 1945. The "night meeting" mentioned in this letter was sacrament meeting. At this time, priesthood meeting and then Sunday School were held in the morning, sacrament meeting in the late afternoon or evening, and auxiliary meetings during the week.

Denver, Colorado
May 21, 1945

Dear Everybody,

Well here it is the 21st of May and the weatherman still doesn't know it's time to turn the sun on. I understand he's sort of messing things up over there, too. Art said Saturday that it was snowing in Zion. He also said they held services for President Grant in the Tabernacle. Did you go? I'll bet there were crowds of people. Hope it was a nice day. Kathie said she sure is glad she's not a President 'cause it seems like all the Presidents are getting dead. When I told Dickie President Grant had died he said "Again?!" Pretty hard for a four-year-old to keep all the dying Presidents straight.

I talked to Bessie for about 15 minutes Saturday on the phone, and was it ever wonderful to just talk to someone who knows some of the same people I know. I wanted her to take a cab and come out to the house for an hour, but she did not feel disposed to. I couldn't go to the station, of course, because there was no one to stay with Dick.

We are so out of gas that I didn't even go to church yesterday. I went to Sunday School on the bus and I would have taken the bus to night meeting but my faith wasn't strong enough to weather the wind and the rain.

I took a bus ride down to Gaylord Saturday afternoon, though, just to get away for a while. The town is green and looks beautiful. The grove of trees across the street on the Seminary grounds looks beautiful and the birds sing over there all day. The lilacs are just breaking out—I saw several bushes Saturday, which makes me feel much better about life in general, although they are very scarce compared with the many in Zion.

Ginny is lying on her back on the footstool kicking her legs and saying "goo, goo" until she gets so excited she can't contain it and then she lets out a crow that you can hear all over the house. She talks to herself all day long and sometimes half the night. Saturday at 11 p.m. after we were in bed we could still hear her gurgling and cooing away. I've given up trying to keep Dickie flat on the bed. He was just about going crazy and so was I. I let him sit out on the sofa for 4 or 5 hours out of the day and I really believe he gets as much rest this way as he does throwing himself around on the bed like a wildcat.

He seems to feel all right but he has this silly fever day after day. Sometimes when he wakes up in the morning it is normal, but by 10 or 11 a.m. it is around 99.2 to 99.6 and hangs there for the rest of the day. I feel a bit discouraged, because if he does have rheumatic fever I know it is likely to be a long slow process and that this fever may continue for several months. I don't see myself getting home for a trip under those circumstances. However, maybe I am too pessimistic. Gordon is much more optimistic than I and feels that he will soon be okay and that we will be able to come home for the Sunday School Board party June 19th. If you happen to be over to Edna's and she has the May issue of "Parents" magazine, Mother, I wish you would read the article on rheumatic fever, and then you will know why I feel fearful. Although he hasn't had blood tests to determine the presence of the disease he has every symptom. Prolonged fever, occasional growing pains, tiredness. Gordon feels that the doctor has not been thorough enough, and that if he actually has something as serious as rheumatic fever the doctor should do more than just jump at conclusions over the phone. When I took him for his check-up 3 weeks after his tonsils were out the doctor didn't take time to listen to his heart and this was the thing we were most concerned about. When I asked about it he just said to have him take it easy and bring him back in 3 months and he would test it at that time. He is so terribly busy; both times I have been to his office the waiting room has been filled and there have been women waiting out in the hall with their children.

Tues. Afternoon

As I was about to say, I would like to bring Dick home sometime this summer and have Dr. S. go over him. Gordon has much more confidence in him. Denver is supposed to have the highest percentage of school children with rheumatic fever of any city in the U.S. Maybe it would be wise to bring him home before another winter rolls around, but these are only thoughts that fly around my mind by day and by night. For the time being, we'll just sit tight and see what happens.

Kathie has been home with a frightful head cold for 5 days and can't seem to get rid of the cough. Of course, in spite of all the precautions I took, Dickie got it, but shook it off in a couple of days. They just don't seem to be able to get acclimated or something. All but Ginny, and she just goes along. But then, of course, she is used to it—being a native Denverite.

The B-29's are roaring overhead like they were having a field day. Maybe it's exam time for them, too. They were at it last night, too long after dark.

I am reading an excellent book (while I feed the baby, 15 minutes, 5 times a day) "Here Is Your War," by Ernie Pyle. Evelyn owes it to herself and her Marine chum to read this book and get a picture of G.I. life in the battle zones. It isn't at all gruesome. Downright funny in places and extremely interesting and enlightening. I'll send it or bring it along when I finish.

I ought to straighten things up now and get supper started. Hope I get a letter tomorrow. Seems like a long time since the last one on Mother's Day, but guess it really isn't.

I hope this letter doesn't sound like a lot of mumping. I have my opinion of people who write home to Mama about every little growing pain, but since I've already done a pretty good job I might as well go all the way. Kathie has a mosquito bite on her ankle that itches like everything and I've got a hangnail on my thumb that's driving me crazy. Otherwise, all is well and I think we can manage. See you before too long, I hope.

Love to everyone,

Marjorie

In the 1940s, effective medicines to treat strep throat were not widely available, and some-times, as in Dick's case, it escalated into rheumatic fever. In the absence of better remedies, the usual treatment was bed rest.

Denver, Colorado
May 29, 1945

Dear Family,

Been trying ever since Sunday morning to get this letter started. I'd make a good sequel to the story of "Pokey Bear."

It was pleasant beyond words to wake up Sunday morning to the tune of Mother's voice. I had about decided when I went to bed Saturday night that I would phone you Sunday after Sunday School, but since you beat me to it, I am enclosing $1 to apply on the bill. I debated all morning after I talked to you whether to send you the $1 or use it to phone Helen, but decided that I would spread things out a bit and phone Helen some other day, rather than talk to everyone on the same day.

Your suggestion that you would come over and stay with Dickie for a week while I go home took me so by surprise that I hardly knew what to say at the time. Gordon has been saying that I should take Ginny and Kathie home just for a weekend. When school is out I think I could get

B. R. to stay with Dick for one day or perhaps even longer. She is about Dorene's age and is very dependable and sensible. Seems to me this would be much less expensive than to have Mother come over, although I would be thrilled to have you come for another stay, so you could see a little of the town, to say nothing of the pleasure it would be to have you here. However, my thought is that if you can come it would be fun for you to come when Helen is here and then we could take in the sights together. I'm thinking, though, that by the time Helen reaches Denver she will be so anxious to get home that wild horses couldn't keep her here for long. My only hope is that she reaches here near a weekend and then perhaps I could arrange to leave the children with Gordon and at least go over for the weekend.

Am sorry Gordon couldn't get hold of Dr. S. when he was there Saturday, as I wanted to find out what he thought of bringing Dickie over for a couple of weeks. I know there is no use asking Dr. B. as he is a fanatic on keeping kids in bed. I'm not saying that he isn't right, because maybe he is, but different doctors have different ideas, and if Dr. S. thought it okay to bring him I would not be afraid to do so. P. B. told Gordon about their neighbor boy who was up and down for a year and a half with rheumatic fever and the doctor finally told his mother to throw her thermometer away and let the boy get outside and play and he's been doing it ever since and seems no worse for it. The fact is, they don't know anything about the darn stuff and every doctor guesses his own way. For the time being, however, I'm going to try to keep Dickie off his feet and resting as much as possible and see how he is by the middle of June. Then I shall write Dr. S. and see about bringing him over. If we get a compartment we could have the bed made up as soon as we get on the train and he could crawl right in and stay until we arrive, so I don't think the trip would tire him too much. My only fear would be having him catch cold, due to the poor ventilation, which might make his temperature rise and bring on another bout of fever, plus rheumatism.

I don't feel too terribly enthused about spending a week over there if Mother would not be home. Not that I wouldn't like to see Daddy and the girls. I'm simply bursting to see them and have them see the baby, but then they would be away mostly in the day and well, you know how it is with Momma. Take away Momma and what have you got? The house seems so darned empty just thinking about it. Guess you should have been twins, Mother, so you could divide yourself up more easily. You're quite all right, what there is of you, but there just isn't enough of you.

The tracing books arrived Monday, Joanne, and they are so clever. The kids just love them and they have surely taken up a lot of time for Dick. All the kids in the neighborhood came in after school to see them and they fell to work on them like a pack of vultures. The paper would all have been used up in 10 minutes if I hadn't shooed them away. Also, thanks for the suckers. The kids felt bad because Gordon forgot to give you the little thing they sent over. He took Mother's slip and another ol' dress of mine that is too short in his briefcase, but said he left the case at the depot, so did not get them to you. Will send them in the mail in a day or two.

You mentioned in one of your letters, Mother, about getting old. Kathie asked me the other day how come you are a "grandma" when you aren't old—so there!

Wonder of wonders! Gordon and I went to church Sunday night *together.* First time since we came here—except when Ginny was named. It was really nice, to be sure. First good look I've had at the town since spring hit, and I must say it looks beautiful. The lawns and shrubs and trees and more trees are lush. The Bonnie Brae district looks elegant.

Here comes Kathie home from school. It's cold and wet, but she's sauntering along with her coat open as if she were afraid she might get here before suppertime.

You mentioned Virginia's *brown* hair. That feather must have thrown you off the track, as there is nothing brown about it. It gets redder every day and *lighter.* The new hair is coming in like a crop of spring carrots. And now I know love is blind because I've never cared for that brand of red hair, but on her—well it looks just as beautiful as if it were coal-black or honey-blond. And it seems to be getting curlier all the time.

Land a goodness—Gordon just phoned to remind me that tomorrow is a holiday. Never once thought of it. I'll have to leave this and get ready to take off for the store as soon as he arrives or we'll have nothing to eat but a wilted piece of celery tomorrow.

Thurs.

Can't say we had a very exciting holiday Wednesday, but it was nice to have Gordon home, he is such a big help with the kids, since he has nothing else to do. We almost decided to wrap Dickie up and go out for a little ride, but got cold feet when it clouded up. He's (Dickie) been lying on the bed all morning threatening me with the worst things he could conjure up. Says if I don't read to him right this minute he'll get right down off the bed and walk right on the bare floor with his bare feet, and he'll go right outside and sit down right on the damp ground.

This morning it was so *hot*. Kathie played out with bare shoulders all morning. By the time she left for school it was so cold she had to wear her woolen skirt, the top part of her snowsuit, and a bandana. Craziest weather I ever saw.

We have radishes in our garden now, peas, beans, lettuce, corn, and tomatoes all perking along. Everyone here is bottling pineapple.

Better get going now. Love and kisses to everyone.

Love,

Marjorie

In August 1945, Marjorie was in Salt Lake with the three children visiting her parents. The United States' victory in Japan was declared on August 14, while she was still there. This meant that the people who owned the Hinckleys' Denver home would be returning, so it was decided that Marjorie and the children would stay with her parents in Salt Lake and Kathie would be enrolled in first grade there. This letter to her husband also refers to his employment dilemma of whether to continue working for the railroad or return to Church employment in Salt Lake City now that the war had ended.

Salt Lake City, Utah
No date, late August 1945
Sunday evening

Dearest,

I really hate to write this letter because my life is so full of sick kids that there isn't much else I can write about and that makes for anything but cheerful reading.

I feel very blue about Dickie. He is getting off to a bad start. That awful croup and bronchial trouble which he had so much of last winter hit him Friday afternoon in less time than it takes to tell it. He was playing on the floor with the baby when all of a sudden he let out with a big bass cough. I put him right to bed with a poultice of Denver Mud and there he has been ever since. His temperature did not go above 100.6, but the cough has been terrific. It wore him to exhaustion on Saturday. Saturday night I kept a steam tent over his bed until 2:30 a.m., and today the cough has been much lighter, his fever is down to 99 and he is better in every way, but is still coughing. Keeping him in bed is hard work and a full time job, but I am trying to be firm.

It will probably be several days before Kathie can start school. I thought her cold was over and done with, but she started with a bad cough today and her temperature is up to 101 tonight. She feels rather miserable and has a white spot on one of her tonsils. I don't like to cross bridges, but I feel in my bones that she will have to have them out before she really gets on top. She is terribly disappointed about missing school, but there just isn't anything that can be done about it. She wants me to go to the teacher and get a list of words so that she will not be behind the other children, and is so concerned for fear she will not be able to go to the first grade until she is 7 years old the way Daddy did, and that does not suit her at all.

When I think of the number of times I have gone to the drug store during the last week I wonder about moving out home [to East Mill Creek] without a car. However, I am not going to think about it until the time comes, as we may know something definite by then. If not, I may order half a ton of lump coal and go out for a week or so. The main problem is bedding. I could use a couple of pairs of sheets or sheet blankets and another pillow or two and perhaps it would be better to buy these and borrow a couple of heavy quilts from the folks, so that we could get along without your having to send anything.

Fall is certainly in the air here. I will do something about your grey suit tomorrow. Getting material will be the biggest problem.

It was good to get your letters this week and they did a great deal for my morale, which is low. I will be glad when we are together, as this setup just does not suit me at all. Grumble, grumble—I knew I should never have started this letter tonight. I'll feel much better after a night's sleep, I miss you and long for you and love you and need you.

No, I'm not overly excited about your having passes on the UP and Santa Fe. I don't see you enough as it is. But as for the job, you had just better make up your mind to do the one which you enjoy the most, as you will spend quite a bit of your life working at it. As for me, I can make myself reasonably happy wherever you are and as for the children, it is a question either way and is something we can not possibly foretell, no matter how we speculate and wonder and worry. I love to think about East Mill Creek at this time of the year, but I suppose Denver is nice in the autumn, too. Is it? You should know. This is your second one there. Imagine that.

Ginny has two teeth!

It is bedtime. I want to get some steam going in the bedroom tonight again and hope that tomorrow everyone will feel better. I sometimes wonder just what is wrong with the way I am caring for these children. I simply can't understand why they should be sick so much. There must be some reason, but I am too tired to figure it out tonight.

I love you, I love you, I love you. Let's hurry and take up life together again. I like it better that way. How about you? Goodnight.

XO

The short separation they had anticipated would stretch clear until Christmas 1945, when Gordon returned to Salt Lake and his work at Church headquarters.

Salt Lake City, Utah
No date, late August 1945

Dearest darling,

This is a terrible life. I've been away from you enough during the last year to last me for the duration of this existence and I hope Heaven is a small place or travel is by instant atomic force.

I had to go to the Board of Education yesterday to get Kathie a registration card, since she is an "out-of-towner." She won't be able to start until Monday because she has the sniffles with a low-grade fever. This cold we just can't seem to get rid of, but keep passing it around and back and forth.

The feel of fall in the air reminds me that I would like a new fall dress 'n hat 'n bag 'n gloves 'n things, but guess I'll just take it easy and brush up my browns, as I spent $10.50 on Dickie yesterday for shoes, house slippers, and zipper sleeping blanket. The blanket works out wonderfully. He was as snug as a bug in a rug all night.

Dickie still has an occasional pain. I am trying to hold him down a bit, but it wears on his disposition until it is hard to live with him.

Hope we get a letter from you today. Take good care of yourself. We all love our daddy.

Marge

Letters to

a Teenage

Daughter

*I*n the summer of 1957, Marjorie was 46 years old, and her children's ages were as follows: Kathy, 18; Dick, 16; Ginny, 12; Clark, 9; and Jane, 3. Gordon, who had not yet been called as a General Authority, was serving as a stake president and employed as an executive secretary of the Missionary Committee, with responsibility for the day-to-day operations of the Missionary Department.

The Hinckleys' oldest daughter, Kathy, took a job that summer at Jacob Lake, a resort in the Kaibab Forest near the Grand Canyon. This section contains letters written to Kathy by her mother during that time.

This was Marjorie's first experience with a child leaving home, and her unique ability to reassure, support, and help her children move toward independence is clear in her letters.

The wedding mentioned in this letter is that of Marjorie's youngest sister, Joanne, to Rey Baird. Joanne was only a few years older than Kathy and was a fourth-grade teacher. The "Cindy" referred to in this and other letters in this section is Kathy's youngest sister, who later decided to be known by her middle name, Jane.

June 10, 1957 (postmark)
Sunday afternoon

Dear Kathy,

After writing you on the yellow paper at Dad's office yesterday we went down to the post office and found a mailbox that could hold the package and so we dropped it in. We figure you should have this by Monday, so if you will try the pink dress and get it back promptly if it will not do, I will get something with a fuller skirt, which will probably fit better. You will notice that I enclosed a spool of pink thread which you can use to take the seams up a little by hand if that is all it needs.

Well, the wedding is now history, but you should see Grandma's front rooms. They are literally stacked with packages. As soon as they get back from their honeymoon they are going to start with it until they are finished or she will not be able to vacuum the front rooms all summer. I think they are going to find it a very wearying task before they get to the end. The wedding was very beautiful. I have never seen Joanne look prettier. The wedding breakfast was held on Bairds' back patio under some spreading trees and it was very lovely. The reception, however, was huge. The bridal party didn't have one moment to relax or catch their breath from 8:30 to 11:15. It was really a killer. Joanne's Sunday School class served and it must have been the first time for some of them in high heels. They nearly died. I had charge of the serving and I have never laughed so hard. Finally at 10 o'clock they all took their shoes off and served in their stocking feet.

They had mailed out 700 invitations and I believe everyone who lived in a radius of 100 miles came. It was mobbed. They ran out of everything—punch, cookies, and ice cream—but they were able to recruit more, so that everyone was served except for about 30 minutes when there were no cookies. A lot of the fourth-grade pupils came, and the little boys made a great point of kissing the bride. They were really cute. They gave her a large silver tray with the inscription: "Miss Pay and Rey, Midvale Fourth Grade, 1957." Her Sunday School class came up to the temple grounds at 9 o'clock the morning she was married and waited outside the gates until they came out at noon, then chased them halfway around the block throwing rice. They decorated the car in lavender and white crepe paper and painted great big ridiculous things all over it and tied tin cans on the back. It was really hilarious. Ginny and Tricia and Deanne and Clark also came up to the temple grounds to help with the rice throwing.

Cindy was so thrilled that she was able to wear her new white dress, which she now calls her wedding dress. The day before the wedding her eye was all swollen with a mosquito bite (they simply poison her) so we had kidded her about having to wear dark glasses to the wedding. Nothing would do then but she must have some dark glasses, so when I brought them home she said, "Oh, thank you, I like them and I promise to wear them to the wedding." When we left home she was so proud of her appearance and she said, "I am just going to enjoy this," and she surely did. However, Dad finally talked her out of the dark glasses before we arrived, as her eye was better and she did look freakish in them. She loved everything about the wedding and Dad could hardly drag her home. Dick got off work at 9:30 and came up, and he and I stayed until 12:30 to help clean up. Joanne and Rey were going to head south on their honeymoon, so if they came your direction instead of Zion's Canyon you might have already seen them and have had her version of all of the above.

I have talked with several girls lately who have not been able to find any summer work, so you can be glad you didn't stay home and try. Your work sounds very interesting and I hope you are enjoying it. I am glad that you like the girls. I felt sure you would.

Dick is going up East Canyon with R. M. tomorrow to try water skiing. The M.'s have a boat up there, and they have been water skiing a couple of times already, so see what you are missing!

We did not get any mail from you Friday or Saturday, so we will surely be looking for the mailman tomorrow. I hope you got the yellow sweater. We had it insured, but we did not insure the package yesterday, so we will be anxious to know if it arrives. I am anxious to hear if you need the red jacket very badly. If so, I will make a real effort to finish it, but if not I will let it skid for a while, as I am so far behind with the ironing, etc., that I need to dive in around here for a few days.

Dad is getting to feel better now, so is anxious to start painting the house, and I should get things in order a little inside so that I can help.

Let us know what telephone service you have down there. We are getting anxious to talk to you unless we can come right after conference. Is there a phone in the lodge? And when would be the best time, and would it be better for you to phone us than for us to phone you? Cindy is always saying with her eyes wide with mystery, "I wonder what Kathy is doing right now."

Dick has just come staggering in from church. They had six speakers and it went way over time. Dad and I are going to the Second Ward at 7 o'clock. Cindy said, "I decided to stay home if the children are staying home." She told Aunt Lois today that she was going to Jacob Lake to get some new shoes.

This is about enough for one Sunday afternoon, so will sign off.

Love 'n kisses,

Mother

This letter to Kathy was purportedly dictated by three-year-old Cindy Jane to her mother.

June 12, 1957
Wednesday, 11:10

Dear Kathy,

She sticked a needle in me. I dot a shot. We doing down and see you and det some new shoes. Thank you for my puzzll. I dot a purse. I thank Dick for the 7-up. I was hungry. I donna wear my wess and my lasses down there. We dotta telephone. We're donna call 'er up. I sleeped in Ginny's bed. My pedal pushers I dot on today. I am witing you a letter, o.k.? I had a picanic with Ginnt. It wasn't down the hollow it was down the Terrace. (Upland Terrace) We had a nice sandwich. We had a hot-dog. I was widing bikes today. I are. I dot my hair tut. I'm donna have it tut aden. That's all. (This is silly, she says.)

Love,

Cindy Jane

The "conference" referred to in this letter was the June Conference that used to be held annually in Salt Lake City for the youth leaders of the Church.

No date, June 1957
Wednesday morning, 7:15 a.m.

Dear Kathy,

This will just be a short note while Dad eats his egg. I thought if I sent it in with him you might receive it a little sooner. The letter that you mailed him last Monday he received at the office early Tuesday morning. And what an interesting letter! Personally, I think you are having a wonderful experience. I would have given anything to have done something similar when I was your age. I should think it would be a real thrill to actually sell something from the curio shop. I can't imagine people buying $100 worth of trinkets in one day. What in the world did you sell? What commission do you get and when do you get it?

I have already thought of several items which were left out of your package. I will try to put a box out for the mailman to pick up today, including your white pedal pushers, your pink T-shirt, and some stationery. I am really embarrassed to send the cummerbund in such a state of disorder. I had intended to fix a bow and streamers, but I was working on it at Grandma's and Evelyn was there with her 6 children. Joanne had all of her gifts displayed out on tables and Evelyn just couldn't keep her little ones out of them, so we had to leave and come home, so I just left the cummerbund with Grandma in an unfinished state. If you really want the bow maybe you can figure out a way to finish it. I was going to wrap a piece of material around the center and then tack two streamers onto the back side of the bow. However, I had the feeling that the bow was too narrow and might not look just right. I suppose the easier thing to do would be to finish putting the hooks and eyes on the cummerbund and let it go at that. What I should have done was just make one long sash to tie around, but it is impossible to piece a sash and have it look right, so I would have had to buy three yards of material and it didn't seem worth the price.

Well, Dad has already gone, so I suppose this letter will go out to the mailbox for pick-up. Our mailman gets here so late in the day that we sometimes wonder if he is coming at all.

This is the strangest summer. With the new job Dick works at installing lockers he leaves on the 4 o'clock bus every day, so he is never here for supper. Last night Ginny went to the beach for an MIA party, Clark was spending the day and night up to R.'s, and that left only Dad and Cindy and me for supper. With no neighbors around either, it is just like a ghost town. While we were eating we read your letter aloud to Cindy. Whenever you mention her in a letter she practically gets hysterical. You mentioned that you couldn't remember that she talked so much, and she thought that was hilarious. She laughed and laughed and laughed. We pacified her for a while by telling her we could go to Jacob Lake in July, but now she says, "I hate July. I don't want to go in July. I want to go this day." I think we all feel about the same. Every morning Dad looks at the calendar and says, "Now, let's see. This weekend there will be too many in the mission home and I'd better be around. Next weekend is conference, etc., etc." It still looks like the week of the 4th would be the earliest we could make it. However, we could not be there until the night of the 1st, which is Monday. Do you suppose you could get your day off on Tuesday, July 2nd, or would that be too close to your 4th of July "rush"? Be thinking about this and we will probably talk to you on the phone before then.

If you could call us on Sunday sometime between 11:30 and 3:30, at least most of us would be home. Around 2:30 or 3:15 we are always here getting ready for 3:30 church, but maybe you are on duty at that hour. Anyway, just phone when you can. Someone is usually here on Sunday at most every hour except Sunday School and church time.

We went to a luncheon at L.'s yesterday. Mrs. R. was there. I asked her how N. was and she said she was having a hard time to keep busy and happy this summer. She was going to have her picture taken and the photographer looked at her and said she would be much more attractive if she had her hair cut first. So he called up some beauty operator he knew and told her just how he wanted it done, and she went over and had her hair all chopped off. When she came back to the studio, he threw up his arms and said that would never do, that the operator had not fixed it like he said and that it was way too short and she would have to let it grow again before he could take her picture. Mrs. R. said when she came home she looked like some kind of a scarecrow. Her hair was short and all piled up in some kind of a set hairdo which just didn't look like her, so she is now hiding behind bushes waiting for it to grow. Oh, the trials and tribulations of hair! By the way, what are you doing with yours these days? Do you wear it up or down, and when do you ever get it washed and dried without being seen by all the public?

There aren't any *light* blue socks around here—only medium blue. Let me know if the ones I sent are too dark. If so, I will have to look in the department stores in town for light blue.

Well, I guess I had better get to the work of the day. Cindy is still sleeping. She has to wait up until ten every night for Dick to get home, so she has been sleeping in. Aunt Lois invited her to the luncheon yesterday and believe me she didn't forget. She just jabbers like a parrot. Last night at dinner when there were just the three of us I don't think she was quiet for 10 seconds. I guess she thought she had to pep things up a little.

I have a case of strawberries to put up and some ironing so I will sign off.

Love to you from all of us,

Mother

Long-distance telephone calls in the 1950s were a luxury, extremely costly by today's standards.

No date, probably June 16, 1957
Sunday

Dear Kathy,

Well, we have just finished talking to you. Anyone would have thought that call was coming from Asia, judging from the excitement. Everyone gathered around and even Dad came staggering out from his nap. Cindy was so excited she could hardly stand still. She talks about you constantly. She is always saying, "I wonder what Tathie is doing right now. Maybe she's having her dinner."

I have been so concerned to know if you are lonely. You have said nothing about the people you work with. When you are in the curio shop, are you there alone? I would imagine the hours would drag there much more than at the fountain. I suppose everyone who comes through the establishment comes to the fountain. Are the cafe and curio shop both in the lodge? With whom do you spend your off-hours?

Four months is a long time to be away, but frankly, I think you are much better off and happier than you would be at home. I talked with C. the other day. Her mother is working all the time and she is taking care of the house. She said she has never been so bored in all her life. K. H. phoned to get your address and she said about the same thing, so I think you are at least having a more interesting time than some.

It is time to get ready for church, so will finish this later. The C.'s have been in Manti for two weeks, but are coming to see us right after church.

Must dash———

8:30 p.m.

We have just been up to give Papa Hinckley a handkerchief for Father's Day. Cindy is getting so she will talk to Aunt Lois now. She told her all about talking to you on the phone.

We don't know what to do about getting down there. I am about ready to take Cindy and start out on the bus. It seems like Dad can never get away. They have the largest group of the year in the mission home right now, so he has to stay around. Then it will be getting ready for stake conference on the 30th. We would like to leave the Monday after, which would be July 1st, but it would be about the 2nd or 3rd when we got there and we were wondering if that would not be a bad time for them to give you a day off, being so close to the 4th of July weekend.

Ginny and Clark wanted to cash in some Green Stamps to get Dad a croquet set or a charcoal grill for Father's Day, but it ended up with Dad buying them one at Grand Central. They have been trying all day to play with it between the rain storms. I have never seen so much rain in this country. I hope it isn't as cold there as it is here or you may be in need of the jacket, which you don't have. I hope you have washed the black and white one by now. Be sure to use a mild soap like Lux or Tide and get it in and out of the water as quickly as possible and then lay it out on a towel until dry.

Dick is giving the lesson in cottage meeting next week.

Ginny said she would write more often but there is nothing happening around here worth mentioning. She says all her life is made up of is dishes and dancing.

It costs us $1.10 to make a person-to-person call to Jacob Lake, but you could call us for 70 cents (reversing the charges) anytime after 7 p.m. or all day Sunday, so don't hesitate to phone us whenever you get the urge. It would probably be better for you to call us, then we will not be bothering you when you are supposed to be working.

I will gather up all these many things you want (with the exception of the bathroom scales) and send them with Grandma. They would like us to drive the Plymouth and go along with them, and Dad is willing for us to do so, but I am a boob about driving all that way without Dad. I will say that travel should be much more pleasant for this family now, however, because as long as Dick is at the wheel he can't be tormenting everyone. The day we rode up the canyon (Decoration Day) he did all the driving and it was so peaceful we could hardly recognize that it was us.

We have surely appreciated you writing so often. We look forward to the mail with the greatest of anticipation. Keep them coming.

Love,

Mother

Kathy would enroll at Brigham Young University in fall 1957, shortly after she got home from her summer job. Box Elder Flats was a canyon picnic site, and Ginny was at the Brighton Beehive girls camp.

August 2, 1957 (postmark)
Wednesday

Dear Kathy,

We received your letter Monday telling about having to speak in church. By this time it will all be history and I am sure you are glad it is behind you. I am sure that your talk was far more listenable than the ones copied out of books. I will be anxious to hear how it went over.

This morning we got up early (and I do mean early) and picked six bushels of apricots. At ten o'clock I went Relief Society teaching and we are getting ready now to go to town. Dick wants to go to Hibbs and buy some shoes at a shoe sale, so far be it from me to prevent him from getting there. At six tonight we are going to the cannery to put up the apricots, so if all goes well the apricots will be out of the way today, except for drying a few later on. Dick is going with me. He would much rather go to the Stake Farm to haul hay with his friends, but it just happened to come on the same night.

Last night was the ward outing at Box Elder Flats. Cindy had a perfectly marvelous time. She loved the community singing and sang as loud as she could. Ginny is still in Brighton so there were just five of us. It seems like we have such a small family all of a sudden, particularly on the nights when Dick works, which is about three or four nights out of the week.

Just when we were getting ready to go last night some boy phoned and asked for you. I told him that you were working in Arizona this summer and so he said he would call you back in the winter sometime. When I asked who was calling he said, "Oh, she wouldn't know me."

We called on H.' s this morning and K. was telling me why she has decided to go to the U. She said every boy that she went out with last winter went to the U, so she didn't see any point in going to school down at the Y and coming home weekends for dates. She thought life in the dorm was a lot of fun, though a madhouse at times. So everyone has his own opinion. It will be interesting to know how it all turns out for you.

We got a letter from the Y saying that the first installment on your room reservation must be in by August 15th or it will be automatically cancelled, so Dad is sending them a check for $55. Well, this is just the beginning. From here on out you can be grateful for Dad's checkbook.

Also, another bunch of literature from the Y says that you must report for registration on a certain date (about September 30th, I think, I'll have to look it up) or pay a late fee.

I am glad M. keeps you supplied with fresh fruit. You had better cultivate that friendship. It sounds to me like it pays off.

This little girl of ours is growing up and getting so self-sufficient it makes me sick. I went in Jr. Sunday School last week and when we got home she said, "Next time I'm going alone. It makes me look like a baby when you go with me."

We made a dash down to Sears one night to get the usual things for Ginny to take to Brighton—new nightgown, new pants, new robe, shower shoes, Levi's, blouse, etc. Cindy nearly drove us crazy begging for us to buy her some school dresses. She said she just couldn't go in all these old shabby ones and she is determined that she is going to school come fall. I don't know how we will ever talk her out of it. She and Clark have been absolutely inseparable all summer. They stick together just like glue, since they have no one else to play with.

Dick gave the 2½-minute talk last week. He didn't read it and it was by far the best he has done.

Ginny went to the beauty parlor, but ended up only having her bangs cut and set like yours. It is a great improvement. She has been determined to have her pony tail cut, but she may change her mind now.

Cindy is developing the most monstrous laugh. Last night Clark inadvertently squirted shaving cream in his face and I thought we were going to have to carry her out. I have never heard anyone laugh so hard. She tried to tell Dad what had happened and she just doubled up.

She is out on the front porch singing at the moment, and I can hear her clear in the TV room. Oh, by the way we had the TV repaired this week, but I don't know why. We haven't found a program worth sitting through yet.

My, you got your skirt finished in short order. Maybe I had better send a little of my sewing your way. Ginny is going to try and get a piece of green material and then she wants to buy one good cotton dress to start school. We might even look at a Lanz. I would like to get her one really good-looking one and then we will make whatever else she needs. She has grown completely out of everything she owns, so she will be starting from scratch and it is going to be a bit tricky to get her fixed up without breaking the bank.

It is time for me to get ready for town, so will close.

We love your letters. Hope to get another one this week.

Mother

P.S. Yesterday Clark was doing something Cindy didn't want him to do. She said, "If you don't stop that I'll just die." He paid no attention but went right on, and she shouted, "Stop that. I don't *want* to die."

I just looked up the registration date. September 26th, 27th, or 28th.

In this letter Marjorie reports telephoning her sister in Heber, Utah, and Gordon's sister in Panaca, Nevada. She also mentions Gordon meeting a young man whom Kathy had been dating at Jacob Lake.

September 8, 1957 (postmark)
Sunday morning

Dear Kathy,

It seems like all I do lately is write letters that never get mailed. They get old and the news is stale, so I burn them and start over.

I was so thrilled when you phoned the other night. I had been wanting to call you all week, but there wasn't anything very special to call about and it seems like a waste of money to just say "hello." We had $6 worth of long distance calls during August, which more than doubled the phone bill, but some of them were to Heber and Panaca, so don't feel disturbed.

About coming home—Dad thinks you should tell the B.'s that you have a chance to ride home if they could let you go early, but tell them that you will stay the full time of your contract if they feel that they need you at all. Of course, I would feel easier if you were riding the bus, but it would surely be nice to have you home a few days earlier than the 20th.

I am really happy that M. came in to see Dad. He is apparently a very bright and capable boy. It is just too bad they couldn't have talked longer, but Dad was on his way to a 4 p.m. meeting. The big push is on for the New Zealand Temple and you know what that means—meetings, meetings, meetings. He went to the temple at 6:30 Saturday morning (yesterday) and is probably going in again this afternoon.

We (including you) are all on Dr. D.' s waiting list to get flu shots, so I thought I would tell you and perhaps you would not be so homesick (if you are). Maybe you have been reading the papers about this Asiatic flu. Dad will get his shot first, as he is on the priority list, since he has a respiratory weakness, but the rest of us will have to wait our turn with the mob.

Everyone is happy in school except Dick. He has been studying geometry every night and he says he simply can't stand this for nine months.

Cindy has just crawled out of bed, so we will get ready and go over to Sunday School. We can hardly wait until you get home. Let us know as soon as you can what you are doing.

Love,

Mother

Letters to

a Sister

The letters in this section were all written to Marjorie's youngest sister, Joanne. At this time, Marjorie's children were beginning to marry and launch careers and schooling, while, on the other end of the spectrum, her parents were feeling the effects of aging. Meanwhile, her husband was called to be an Assistant to the Twelve in April 1958 and was ordained an apostle in October 1961. The rhythm of their life together was changing dramatically. Marjorie's sister, who lived in Germany and later in Indiana, was evidently a great sounding board and confidante. In turn, Marjorie offered encouragement and support to her loved ones far away.

At this time, it was common for boys graduating from high school to enlist in the armed forces for six months of active duty, followed by a period in the reserves.

December 11, 1958

Dear Joanne,

I am at Gordon's new office. I have been Christmas shopping, I mean looking, and am waiting for him to get out of a meeting so we can go home and feed our brood.

Our home typewriter is broken, so you can only hope to hear from me when I am able to steal a few minutes at the office. I forgot my long-hand years ago.

Well, we all had one good laugh after Dorene read your letter to Mother with the great big secret. We just tried to keep Mother laughing for as many days as we could and kidding her about having a baby-sitting job in Germany next July, etc., etc., and etc. She really took it pretty well, although she has now had time to worry about your getting up and down the three flights of steps, and the hospital bill, and millions of other little items that I am sure will all be taken care of in due time just as if you had good sense. The only thing that worries me is that if you have a boy he cannot qualify to be President of the United States, being born outside the country. However, if it *is* a boy he might someday go back to Germany and visit his birthplace on a mission or something and it could make life very interesting. I am sure you will get along just fine, and this will only make your experience there more memorable and meaningful than it could ever have been otherwise.

Dick passed the physical for the army and will be sworn in tomorrow. This means he will probably go to Fort Ord next June if he is lucky, and that should get him home for Christmas—next Christmas, that is. That will give us one more year to work on his bedroom—the rush is on. He is going in with his best friend and the bishop's son, also a good friend. The outfit is mostly LDS and he feels quite happy about it, so it should work out fine.

Mother went to Ogden today to help Dorene get some cleaning done in preparation for moving this Saturday. They hope to be all settled for Christmas. This means we will have to dig up a few more funny jokes to keep Mother smiling, but she will get used to it in time. Dorene has promised to come down once a week, so actually it should be a very nice arrangement.

Keep the news about your sweet adorable little daughter coming. Mother reads us every word about her. We miss you all very much, but wouldn't have it otherwise. This may not be the most fabulous Christmas you have ever had, but it will be one you will remember when all the rest are forgotten. Love to all three of you.

As a General Authority, Elder Hinckley was assigned to visit stake conferences every weekend except in July and part of December.

January 25, 1959
Sunday

Dear Joanne, and Rey and Charlene,

I borrowed your typewriter while ours is being repaired to type my Relief Society lesson, so before returning it will use it to write a few lines. I did scratch one out in longhand a week ago, but the news is so old it is worthless.

Thank you so very much for the darling Hummel. I really like the one you chose. It is just darling. The girls both love it and are going to try to send you some money to buy one for them. Also, the picture blocks were a huge success. They stole the show on Christmas. Everyone from Dick on down tried their hand at them. Ginny and Kathie went simply wild over them because they thought they looked so "European." You should not have spent money on us this Christmas, but since that is water under the bridge we surely thank you for everything.

Our Sundays have settled into a new pattern. Gordon is usually away, I mean *always* away, and the rest of us are always home watching the clock so we won't be late for church. Gordon is in California today and is coming home Western Pacific in the morning. I think I will take Mother in the VW and drive up to Ogden to meet him. It will save him a bus ride down and give us a chance to call on Dorene for a minute. I have seen her just once since Christmas. Her husband seems to be very well pleased with his job and I believe they are going to be quite happy up there. He spoke in their sacrament meeting a week ago. That was his first experience to speak in a sacrament meeting. Dorene said he did extremely well and she was so proud of him.

Dick has joined the United States Army. Each Monday night he goes to drill and then comes home and simply kills us dead with his imitations of life with Sergeant Bilko. I wasn't at all thrilled with his decision to "join up," but I find that 17-year-old boys pretty much do as they please, and since he seems to be with his friends in a fairly good outfit I suppose it is all right. If he is lucky his outfit will go to Fort Ord in June and will be through in time for winter quarter 1960. If peace prevails he should be able to get through school with only this one interruption, so that will not be too bad.

Gordon had an assignment in Mesa two weeks ago. We took Clark and Cindy and had a very nice vacation (if you can call it that) from Friday until Monday. It was one of the nicest trips we have ever had. The weather down there was just like spring, a nice warm 75 degrees. We stayed in a lovely motel and had a lovely chicken dinner at the home of the stake president after the afternoon meeting and then left immediately for home. The people treat you so wonderfully when you go to their conferences that it makes you feel very humble, and very, very undeserving. He has an assignment to the other Mesa stake on February 8th. I guess he will have to drive again as the train service to Mesa is such that one has to go to L.A. and back.

It is time to get ready for church. More later.

I imagine that the next six weeks will be rather tedious for you, as the weather should be a bit chilly and I suppose you will be pretty much housebound. I wish you could arrange some way to get a car by spring so you could get around and see the country. Switzerland should be a thing of beauty in the spring. Gordon and Dick are simply mad about this little VW. If we had the money we would send it to you to buy another and then sell this one we have next fall. Somehow you must arrange to get a car, even if you have to rent one. How is the used car market? Is there anything available or does everyone drive his car "until death do ye part"? After seeing all the old cars in use in Europe I would wonder if there is ever one for sale.

We are still trying to get this old shanty fixed up. Little by little we are dabbing paint around, but no big changes ever seem to take place. I have plans to paint the hall this week. We have the new wallpaper bought, so the next thing will be to put that on. Next week Gordon's assignment is in town so we made big monstrous plans for Saturday, but only to find out that the stake to which he is assigned is being reorganized, which means interviewing men all day Saturday. This weekend business is just relentless. I had no idea how constant some things can be—just like the sun coming up and going down. At least, it ought to give one a feeling of security in the pattern of things.

The three dollars enclosed is for you to buy Rey a birthday present. I have your name this year for birthdays, so if you will relay this to him with our best wishes I will be glad. It is late, as usual, because I didn't know until yesterday that I had your name.

Kathie is talking of coming to Germany again. She would like to come and stay with Charlene while you go to the hospital and we would love to send her if the ticket were not so expensive. She wants to work spring quarter, so she can come in June, but I am sure it is out of the question.

Kiss Charlene for us,

Love,

Marge

Dear Joanne,

Mother just read to me your letter telling about your recent travels. It takes me back over a beautiful dream. I am glad you went to Italy. Weren't you thrilled with the statue of Moses! That is the only work of art that has ever brought tears to my eyes. I will be anxious to hear how you liked Copenhagen. I understand it is a very beautiful city and I wanted so much to visit it last year, but Gordon was more anxious to come home via Madrid, so I keep telling myself that we will include Copenhagen the next time. It is a silly thing that once you have seen any of Europe you have to keep telling yourself that you will be back again or you would be perfectly miserable.

I suppose Mother keeps you posted on the small talk around here. Our life remains about the same, very busy, but nothing to complain about. We are moving into our new church building this week. I feel some nostalgia at leaving the old church on the bend, and to be out of walking range will be an inconvenience, but it will be nice to be able to elbow into a Sunday School class without getting claustrophobia. If they divide our ward we will be on the far west end and will feel very much on the fringe.

I hope if you are planning any more trips you could visit Einsiedeln, Switzerland. This is a Catholic stronghold up in the mountains where they house a magnificent panorama painting of the Holy Land which makes you feel that you are standing right at the foot of the cross. It is one of the most impressive experiences I have ever had. You might look into it. We made the loop from Berne up to Lucern then to Einsiedeln and through the most beautiful valleys of the Alps, including the valley of Lauterbrunnen, which in my opinion is the most typical and breathtaking scenery of Switzerland. When you have made this circuit I will be satisfied that you have seen Switzerland at her best. Hope you can make it.

Gordon's schedule of conferences is very tiring. I like it less each weekend. He is leaving for Pocatello on Friday morning this week and next week he leaves on Thursday for Los Angeles. However, last Sunday he was in Mill Creek Stake and had his first Sunday dinner at home in almost a year. It was just like a vacation.

The page is filled, so will get along with the semiannual cleaning of the garage. If you cannot decipher this you haven't missed much. At least you know we are thinking of you. We love to hear about Charlene. Surely miss her—and you too, but have fun and stretch it out as long as you can afford to.

Love,

Marge

August 4, 1959

Dear Joanne, and Rey, Charlene and Elaine,

We enjoyed your letter from the hospital and were so happy that you had good care and that you have another sweet little girl. It is hard to imagine her existence. Try to send a picture when you can.

If I told Dorene you had not written to us it was only a passing remark and *not* a complaint. I can think of no more *unprofitable* way to spend a year abroad than writing letters home. As long as Mother gets a word from you every week, everyone is happy. We can, and do, get the news from her, so you needn't feel any obligation to answer what few letters you might receive from me. Forgive me, however, if you have written us and I failed to give you full credit.

I feel as if I had been on vacation all summer, as Ginny has kept the house cleaned and Dick has helped so much in the yard. If he could have stayed home another month the old homestead would have taken on a "new look." However, he accomplished quite a lot in the six weeks he had—a sprinkling system for the backyard, all the former garden space planted in lawn, two new rock and cement paths, and various repair jobs too numerous to mention. Needless to say, I feel as if my "right arm" was gone since he left.

Suppose Mother told you that we drove him to Fort Ord—had a nice 2 days in San Francisco with all the family before driving down, and then came home through Yosemite. We get wonderful letters from him, and though the going is a little rough he seems to be taking it in good stride.

Gordon has had a six-week vacation from stake conferences—next Sunday ends the lull and then he will be back on the circuit. It was surely a treat to sit in a Sunday School class with him for the *first time* in 22 years of matrimony.

They just divided our ward and I have not felt so strange since moving out here as a bride. I can only name about 10 people—the rest are all young couples who have moved into the subdivisions during the past year. I am going to continue with the literary lesson in Relief Society. Kathie is coordinator of the Jr. Sunday School and Ginny plays the music.

Kiss your new little one for us.

Love,

Marge

P.S. to the baby:

Clark is so worried that you will be a German, but Ginny says how "neat" it will be for you to be able to fill all the "place of birth" blanks with "Heidelberg," so I guess it's all in the way you look at it. Tell your mother to send us all the details about you, so we can believe you are real. Love and kisses from all of us.

Auntie M

P.S. to Joanne:

Remembering my experience when Gin was born in Denver I know how homesick you will be to show her off to your family and friends, but don't let it throw you.

Love,

M

P.S. to the baby's big sister, Charlene:

We saw a colored snapshot of you last night. You look so grown up and so different from the way we remember you. Grandpa was sure your hair is red from the pictures, but I think it is most likely just the colored film that makes it look so. We like the new name you chose for the baby. How is your German coming? Cindy gets very exasperated because Dick writes letters to her in German.

Love,

The Hinckleys

Several years have passed, and Joanne's family has moved to Indiana.

April 15, 1965
Thursday

Dear Joanne,

I didn't know how to answer your letter about Mother and Daddy coming to see you, as I really couldn't tell what their real feelings were without talking to each one of them alone. This I finally accomplished yesterday. I had an "appointment" with Daddy while Mother was at Relief Society. They are both very anxious to come, but full of misgivings over whether they should or not, because of the money and because you are planning to be home this summer, etc., etc., etc. However, I think we have settled their fears and as of now they have decided to come as soon as Katherine leaves, which would mean they would leave here about Tuesday or Wednesday, May 4th or 5th. They will probably take the nonstop jet to Chicago, which puts them in the big city about 11:10 a.m. We would like them to take the plane from Chicago to Bloomington, but have not yet checked on what flights are available. They should know this by Sunday when you call.

One of these days I will sit down and write all the "small talk," but I am under a little pressure today, so will postpone it. Things are still going full steam around here. Dick is well into his major of economics and has only had one B since he got into this field. He seems to have hit his stride.

Ginny is still "madly in love" and is talking about a September wedding. At this point, she is still talking about graduating, even though she has two more years. He will work on his Master's in zoology next year and perhaps change to medicine the following year.

Must dash—take good care of yourself and your adorable little brood. We loved the pictures. Wish you could send more. Hope Rey is enjoying his school.

Love,

M

Virginia, the Hinckleys' third child, was married in 1965, and Clark was beginning school at BYU. With four of the five children out of high school by this time, Marjorie had more opportunity to become involved in family history work.

September 29, 1965
Wednesday

Dear Joanne,

Congratulations! I don't know why it should have made any difference at all but we were delighted she turned out to be a "she." Rebecca is one of my favorite names. The only reason we didn't give it to Jane was that our neighbors used it the month before. I guess we were saving it for you. It goes so beautifully with Baird. It was nice of you to wait until you got home. Just barely! My, you live dangerously! It was good for Mother and Daddy to talk to you Monday. Daddy has his up and down days and he didn't bother to get out of bed that day until they put the call through to you. Then he stayed up for the rest of the day. Sometimes it takes a few less pills and a little more incentive.

I could scream! I forgot to have you check over this biography of Daddy's while you were here. It seems like a lot to ask of you with 5 little ones, but nonetheless I am sending it to you next week. Then at least you cannot say you didn't have a chance. If you get time to make some additions and corrections, please do so. I hope to start on Mother's life next week.

It was *so wonderful* to have you here for the wedding. Still can't believe we could have been so fortunate. Thanks for everything you did to make it complete. The kids went to Carmel for a week and had a wonderful time, then had a week at home to clean up the chaos. It was so bad they had to spend the first night in a motel.

Everyone is back in school. Ginny is so *busy* preparing those 3 meals a day she has no time to talk to us. Kathy is just screaming with laughter.

Clark came home for a missionary farewell the first weekend, but made it clear that he had never had so much fun in his whole life and would not be home again until he *had* to—of course, this was at the end of orientation week. I think he's not quite so enthralled with it since class work began. He has 18 hours and is in the Honors program and I suspect it is interfering with his sleep. He's strictly a 9 o'clock boy.

We are down to 2 children and I'm making a terrible adjustment. I spend all day counting my blessings while I'm licking my wounds. I've been talking up BYU to Jane, but I suddenly realized that would leave us with no chilluns at all so there's got to be some other way.

I'm writing this during Relief Society General Conference in the Tabernacle. The meeting this morning was fabulous and the afternoon session is now under way so I'll end the letter writing.

We are happy and grateful you have your little girl here safe and sound.

Just wish we could drop in and see her. Fill us in on all the details whenever you can and keep those 4¢ post cards going to Mother and Daddy!

Love to all,

M

Dear Joanne,

I hope the U.S. Government will honor this old aerogramme. I happened to have this and I do not happen to have an 8¢ stamp, so I'll take a chance.

What a dreamer! When I saw that Gordon's next appointment was in Fort Wayne I just turned my head and tried not to think about it. Wives must pay their own transportation to stake conferences, unless they are overseas. Consequently, I never go to stake conference unless they are driving cars, and this is almost a thing of the past since jet service was invented. It wouldn't be quite so hard if it were not for the new little Rebecca, but it surely is hard to miss seeing her. Like Kathy always says—she only wants money for one reason and that is travel. This week I could heartily agree with her. But right now $200 for a weekend trip is not in my budget. There is a possibility that his assignment will be changed from Fort Wayne to Kanab because of a military problem in that town and I am almost hoping it will be changed, then I will not feel so sorry for myself. It would be lovely, wouldn't it? To see you in Fort Wayne, I mean.

I will not send the copy of Daddy's life until after Christmas, as I want to make an extra copy so as not to take a chance of losing it in the mail. I could never face having to do it over again. Like Carlyle, every word is written in "blood and sweat." It's a good thing I don't have to earn a living manufacturing words—written words, that is.

It is a bit ridiculous to think you would receive a copy of Grandma Pay's life in a fast hurry, but there is one thing about us, we always have valid excuses. My copy was missing page 9 and it has taken me all this time to get it from Mother and copy and insert it. But it has now been accomplished and I am putting it in the regular mail today, so look for it in four or five days.

Things are about the same with Daddy. Mother is doing a little better. Not quite so weepy over everything, especially if we can get her out rather often. She goes to a D&C class with me each Friday, and with an occasional cousin's club and Relief Society she gets around enough to keep her from getting too melancholy. Daddy started the D&C class with us and paid his $6.00 for the course, but only lasted through two weeks. He doesn't feel like going anywhere lately. Just content to stay home. The cold, foggy weather makes a difference, and it is such an effort for him to get out that we don't push him too hard. Although it is the old story—the things that really interest him, he has the strength for. He was as chipper as could be for his birthday party, and enjoyed it immensely, and by the way, we surely did miss you and the tribe for the occasion. It was incomplete without you, but the letter you sent to Daddy was worth a million.

We each had a cry over it, because you expressed what each of us feels, but could not put into words. Nothing you could have done for Mother and Daddy could possibly have made them so happy. Daddy said that letter made his whole 80 years worthwhile, and I am sure he meant it. Bless you for doing what we all should have done, but didn't. With your permission, or without it, we are going to have it printed and attached to his history for the genealogy books.

Not out of things to tell you, but I'm out of paper, so will close. Give that little Rebecca a kiss for all of us, and how about some pictures. Have you taken any of her? Please pass them along!

Love to all of you,

Marge

Letters to
a Growing
Family

*I*n this, the longest section of letters, we get a clear picture of the day-to-day life of the Hinckleys. The children were grown and beginning to have children of their own, and Marjorie kept them all up to date on each other and on the happenings of their family. The teamwork of a husband and wife in everyday living is evident here. From yard work to social engagements to Church assignments, they supported each other and worked together.

The Hinckleys at this time had moved from East Mill Creek to their new home on Ensign Downs, on the hill north of the state capitol building. Their daughter Kathy, to whom most of these letters are addressed, was living in Hawaii with her family.

One of the appealing things about these letters is the unremarkableness of the accounts. Despite the unusual circumstances of this particular family's existence, many of the things they grappled with are the concerns that affect us all: planting gardens, cleaning house, studying lessons, worrying about children. These letters help us see that—for all of us—much of life is lived in the quiet corners of daily activity, moving forward a step at a time.

Four generations of Hinckley women. Clockwise from top: Virginia Hinckley Pearce, Marjorie Pay Hinckley, Elizabeth Olsen, Catherine Olsen, and Rosemary Pearce Olsen

Clark and his wife, Kathleen, had been in Salt Lake for a summer visit and were returning to Clark's job in Manhattan. Jane and her husband, Roger, had purchased the Hinckleys' old home, which they all referred to simply as 3703. The wives of the General Authorities gathered for lunch each month, an event Sister Hinckley referred to in her letters as "Wives' Luncheon." Because General Authorities traveled to stake conferences every weekend, Monday was typically their day off.

August 27, 1975
Thursday

Dear Kathy,

They are using a jackhammer on the brick walk today to take the whole thing out, cement base and all. This will be the third time for the cement base and the second time for the brick. It is like Ginny said, she thought it was pitiful that we had to wait for Dad to do everything instead of hiring a crew, but now she would be only too delighted if Dad would take over her wallpaper hanging and a few things. I am sure he could do a better job on the brick walk than the experts have come up with yet, and I am beginning to think it might have been faster. After all, this has been going on since June.

Sunday was "cry" day. Clark left at 7 a.m. I didn't have a driver's license, so I spent the day feeling sorry about just everything. However,

Dad got home around five and we drowned our sorrows by staring at the brick walk and discussing possible solutions.

Monday he was home all day. We went out to 3703 to measure up the shower and then bought one like yours. When it will get installed is another story.

Wednesday was high-society day. Went to a luncheon at the Alta Club with 50 other lovely ladies to honor A. M. It is a good thing I wore my very best dress and jewelry. Tuesday night went to the annual *Church News* staff feast and it was a real feast. How can one be a Mormon and not wrestle with the weight problem?

On Tuesday I rode the bus to Ginny's and sewed on a button or two on the school clothes. The only one who gets anything new is Rosie. The others just shift down one.

I whipped my house into shape this morning, as I had before-noon callers. Just what I need every day. They came to see what I had that could be used to decorate the tables at the Wives' Luncheon next week. The program will be reports on the Asian conferences. I get to do the one on Manila. Hope I can pack it into 7 minutes.

Am having 18 people here to lunch tomorrow and must get out and rustle the groceries immediately, as we are going to Provo tonight where Dad speaks to the faculty.

Aloha—and love,

Whenever possible, on a Church assignment, the Hinckleys would stop en route to visit their children in various parts of the country. Here Marjorie is hoping for a stopover in Hawaii. She and her husband had attended a reception honoring Emperor Hirohito and Empress Nagako of Japan in San Francisco the day before this letter was written.

October 11, 1975
Sunday

Dear Kathy,

I have been waiting for our plans to fill before writing, but you know Dad. It seems he has to be in Tokyo a few days earlier than the seminar to meet with David Kennedy on a property problem. He may have to take a non-stop from S.F. to Tokyo w/ no stopover in Hawaii in order to get there in time. Don't know what I am doing. Would like to get away Wed. morning but the way things look now, it will probably be Thurs. Will call you around six p.m. (your time) either Tues. or Wed. If Dad goes non-stop to Tokyo I will meet him there in time for the seminar.

This weekend got completely wiped out. Dad had to speak at a funeral at noon and then go directly to Magna. I spent the afternoon at the dentist. Monday Dad flies to St. George for the public opening of the Temple. That wipes Monday out and our last chance to get anything done around the house. It turned cold and poured rain the day after you left. Between the weather and trying to help Ginny get her apples and pears in bottles the tulip bulbs still sit in the garage.

The luncheon for the Emperor in San Francisco yesterday was a beautiful affair in the St. Frances hotel. I'd forgotten what an exciting place San Francisco is. Sister T. and I walked through Gumps for a few moments before going over to the hotel. What window shopping!

I am writing this letter at the Magna Stake house at 8 a.m. Sunday morning. I always like to come to the reorganization of a stake because I never get called on to speak and can relax and enjoy it.

We dashed out to 3703 early Saturday morning as Roger was pruning the forest and Dad had to be sure it was done just right. Jane was on her hands and knees scrubbing the basement steps. I never get over the wonder of it all.

It seems that Dad is going to reorganize 3 stakes in Tonga on his way to Australia in November. That might be something for you to think about, as the Saturday of a reorganization is always free time for me while they are interviewing.

Gin still had her conference visitors as of yesterday. Their car broke down.

Will be talking to you soon. Love to all.

M

P.S. If you think you are miscast in the Cub Scout program, try this on your violin—Dad has just been made adviser to the Tabernacle Choir.

The United States was celebrating its 200th birthday, and talk of bicentennial celebrations filled the year.

February 5, 1976
Thursday

Dear ones,

Well, we did it again! Got Dad packed up and on the way with not too many casualties. He had to jump off the plane before takeoff to give one more message to his secretary and then make a phone call on a matter and is now ready for the long hop to Tokyo. Three inches of snow in Salt Lake this morning and I had to take Dad down the hill at 6:15. Drove back up State Street sideways, but made it without further fender dents.

There is really no big news from the home front, but since I am under the dryer at the hairdresser and have read all about the new Mrs. Onassis during past sittings I will scratch out a quick note. I still miss the intimacy of the little ol' Z.C.M.I., but must admit the new store is beginning to look like Saks Fifth Ave.

Went on the swing shift at the cannery last night to get 2 cases of pineapple. Got home at 2 a.m. Want to keep up the tradition of doing everything the hard way. Jane went with her ward and all the old ladies last week. She thought it was a ball.

Winter is with us again, but we have crocuses and daffodils blooming in our courtyard, which of course makes Dad the world's greatest horticulturist. Must admit it is pretty exciting, what with the snow still on the front lawn.

The girls see no way to get the family Bicentennial under way for April. More time is needed. Surely you will have to come back in May, June, or July to meet other commitments, or if needs be it could be postponed 'til Oct. conference time.

Sent R. S. material. The booklet of vignettes is to be used each week during opening exercises, but since you are not R. S. president this may be useless. Ginny says the music stores have a whole section of Bicentennial music which is terrific, also short plays for children. If the Hawaiian music stores are not so equipped you might want her to send you something.

Dad gave a Bicentennial talk at Gin and Jim's fireside Saturday night and did a super job.

I've been cleaning Mother's closet and have found some treasures: the black velvet stole Mary Goble wore for years and 2 of your storybook dolls.

Love,

M

Kathleen, Clark's wife, was two classes short of finishing her university degree when they got married. Now, with one child born and another on the way, she was trying to complete those last classes.

March 26, 1976
Friday morning

Dear Kathy,

While Holly is asleep I'll dash off a line. Kathleen has gone to the library to study this morning. It's much easier to discipline oneself there than at home. She is to have a test in anatomy tonight. On Wednesday, Clark had to drive her over to the hospital emergency in the middle of the night where they gave her a shot and that gave her almost immediate relief. But in the meantime they were so excited about checking her in and getting her breathing that they locked the keys in the car. Then they walked home carrying Holly in the cold night air only to find that the house keys were with the car keys. They broke the front door glass to get in. It could have been worse—a policeman could have come along and arrested them for breaking into a house at 3 a.m. I think when she gets this school bit over it will help the asthma. She has been under a lot of pressure.

The material for my dining chairs came yesterday and it is a total disaster. Won't do, at all. I needed you to pick it out. Now to find something that is available locally so we can get it on for conference is going to be wild. I wouldn't worry about conference, except that we will have the Asian Saints here again and it is a little tricky to have 40 people without chairs. We discovered on our last trip that they look forward to food at the Hinckley home after the last session of conference.

I am enclosing Ginny's diet. Misery likes company. I stayed on it for 10 days and ended up with divertic. Too much roughage for my delicate insides. The melba toast you can buy in the package is only 16 calories, compared to 68 calories for a slice of toast and will sometimes suffice when one is bread hungry.

Your letter came yesterday. Dad got it first and we were in literal physical combat to see who would read it first. Glad your garage sale was a success and that the project is behind you. I was horrified over the estimate of $5,000 for your bed-and-bath addition. I was thinking in terms of $1,200, but Dad reminded me that a bathroom alone can cost $3,000 or $4,000. Hope you get started soon and that the handy man stays on 'til the bitter end.

What is with this boy thing with your girl? Utterly disgusting at the 6th grade level. Maybe you had better paint some freckles on her face and black out a front tooth. Glad to hear you are involved in the school again. This should make the girls feel like the good old days are returning.

Best move right along now while Holly is sleeping.

Love,

The Hinckleys had just returned from a Church assignment in Asia. Whenever she returned from a trip, Marjorie tried to contact the parents of the missionaries she had met. The "Windsors" were a group of men who had served with President Hinckley in the British Mission and their wives, who met socially on a regular basis.

May 11, 1976
Tuesday

Dear ones,

All the mental plans I made about diving into the work schedule when I got home have been frustrated through lack of energy. I plan the kind of days I used to be able to execute at age 30 and find I cannot now live up to my expectations. However, it is good to be home and to do a little puttering. It took me three days to lift the lid of my suitcase and empty out the Hong-Kong-smelling contents.

The first day home was a total wipeout, since it was Saturday and Dad was saying, "Marge, come here and look at this." Then there was the hair appointment and a formal dinner at night. About the only thing accomplished Saturday was a sizing up of all the horrendous projects that need doing around this yard and house immediately. I keep telling myself that once we get the house finished and the yard in it will be different. We have the Windsors in two weeks and I had hoped that would be the deadline for the bookcases, but Dad has only one thing in mind and that is the yard. The weeds had taken over in the front except where the lawn is. Another load of topsoil has been dumped in the driveway and everything in the courtyard is dead, except the shrubs. Roger and Jane are screaming for help on their bathroom, so we spent a couple of hours there on Saturday, also.

Sunday Dad went to the temple and then Ginny invited us to dinner, which was super great, as I have not yet done any grocery shopping. I think that happens this afternoon.

Monday we worked in the yard until noon when Dad had to go to the office. Then he spotted a furniture sale and I had to check that out. I bought two matching floor lamps for the front room.

Ginny wants me to participate in her Relief Society lesson tomorrow. It is on friends and she wants me to tell about how travel isn't all that great in and of itself, but it is the friends along the way. Since I have to go there tomorrow I thought I would skip ours today, since I felt too pressured to do 2 Relief Societies in one week. This morning our Relief Society president phoned to see if I would give the opening prayer and I nearly tripped over my tongue trying to make being "too busy" sound reasonable.

Everyone seems to be fine. The pregnant women are a little more so, but the miracle story is that Dick has not had one sniffle since the kenalog shot.

Thank you for a wonderful time. You lost a week completely and I trust that you will be able to make it up without too much stress and strain.

I am still calling parents of missionaries, but my main project today is to get some bedding plants in the courtyard.

Yours truly,

M

June 3, 1976

Dear ones,

I have spent 11 hours during the past two days pulling, yanking, digging, jerking, spading to get rid of all the glorious mint we planted in our front yard the first summer. It has become an obnoxious weed in an ugly purple color and is choking out all other more worthy shrubs and ground coverings. My hands are so swollen I cannot wear my rings and my back feels like a worn-out rubber band. As a result of all of this tremendous physical exercising I have not had the strength to write you a letter. But today is my day of R and R. I put on my nylons at 7:30 this morning and went to the hairdresser and for a load of groceries, and will be on my way to Wives' Luncheon as soon as I put a little polish on my broken-down fingernails.

Last Friday night we attended the 50th LDS High School reunion. What a hoot! They took over the entire hotel. People came from Florida to California as it included all those who had ever attended LDS High until it was closed in 1931. The boys who sat at the head table were announced as they entered the ballroom with all spotlights turned on them while they took their places. Dad was right up there with George Romney and the old student-body presidents. In fact, they invited him to give the opening prayer. Dinner was served to 840 bald-headed men and fat women. There was one couple from the class of 1905. I sat next to the student-body president from 1924, who was the master of ceremonies, and never have I sat by such an adorable, charming dinner partner. The dinner commenced at 7:30 and the program did not end until midnight. The later the hour got, the happier and noisier everyone became. It was a gala affair. Dad, who didn't want to go in the first place, had the time of his life. He was the little bashful boy who had made good.

Saturday night we went to the Bicentennial performance of the Tabernacle Choir and Utah Symphony. First time they had appeared together. It was mostly original music. We were both exhausted from working outside, and those benches get mighty hard by 10:15.

Sunday we had a nice quiet day. Went to our little own fast meeting in Capitol Hill 2nd Ward and it was lovely. Such a variety of interesting people who live on Capitol Hill.

Dad and K. have a couple of projects up their sleeves. One is to brick both of our driveways and the other is to glass in the decks for a greenhouse. But right now I will settle for getting the yard squared away. We still have a lot of planting to do, but it won't get done for a couple or more days, as tonight Dad has to prepare a talk for LDS Business School graduation. Friday he has to give the talk and Saturday is a funeral. E. C.'s widow died unexpectedly in her sleep. When I saw her a few weeks ago she was perking right along so I was surprised to hear she had gone. She was one adorable lady whom I will miss. It has only been six months since Brother C. died, so I guess you could say it is quite nice.

Dad keeps saying that I am going to Washington, D.C., with him on the 4th, but Jane is really nervous about it, so if it looks like she is close to delivery I will not go. I would be so happy to have Celia come as soon as she can. She could be a big help in tending Holly and Jennie and Michael, and it would be so great just to have her lovely person with us for awhile. Kathleen and the Pearces are excited at the prospect also. If she would not be too homesick and if you could function without her I hope you will consider it.

More later,

Mother

June 3, 1976
Thursday night

Dear Kathy,

When I returned from Wives' Luncheon here was the letter from you. Though I had mailed one to you this morning I decided I would answer immediately, as I am kind of in limbo tonight. Too tired to begin any projects. I will have tomorrow morning to whisk through the house and then go to the funeral and by that time the weekend will be upon us.

Imagine buying wallpaper at a garage sale! How terrific! Sounds like the making of a super beautiful room. How about the fabric for your bamboo chairs? Any decisions yet? They returned our chair (the white one with the turquoise seats). The pink velvet on the back and the crewel on the front is simply elegant, but the cushion is too large for the chair and we are in the process of trying to have it redone. It is never ending.

Can't imagine all those goings on for graduation. I certainly must keep my savings account in good shape. Dad is dragging his feet on getting the necessary shrubs to finish up the yard so I decided I would take $100 of my savings and go down to the nursery and get the job done. This business of waiting for a sale on euonymus is for the birds. K. has promised to send a boy to help on either Saturday or Monday.

Life for your girls sounds just great. I hope you are getting pictures. This is a colorful interlude in their growing-up experience. We got a kick out of your description of Heather being whisked away by a casanova in white pants. I know how you must have felt.

Tomorrow Gin is giving a book review on *Mary Fielding* at her book club. She didn't begin to prepare it until today, but when I called tonight she said she had it all in shape and was going out to the pool to have a swim. Ah, youth!

I will still try to put together a Bicentennial family party, but will not get going on it for another couple of weeks, as I am obsessed with getting the yard planted at the present. I have a one-track mind.

The June wedding invitations are pouring in. My budget is going to look sick.

Love to all,

Mother

In 1976 the Teton Dam in Idaho burst and many people's homes were wiped out.

June 8, 1976
Tuesday

Dear Kathy,

Saturday we went out to Jane's again to work on the shower. It has become a monumental task. We thought we were getting rid of the old house, but not so. When we got home I had left a pan of spaghetti with hamburger boiling away on the stove. The house was full of thick air and pungent smell. I was feeling terrible about the whole thing when I opened the garage door from the kitchen and found that Dad had pulled the hose inside with the spray sprinkler on and had absent-mindedly turned on the tap. Water was hitting the ceiling and spraying from wall to wall to wall. I simply cracked up. We looked at each other in total disbelief and wondered whatever was going to become of us.

We opened up the windows, swept out the water, and decided to get away from it all by going over to see Clark and Kathleen and getting some groceries. While en route I was seized with a sudden attack of divertic and hardly made it through the checkstand. By the time I got home and into bed I was having chills and fever and so much pain I was trying to decide just what I wanted included in my obituary. Dad called everyone and told them the invitation to Sunday dinner was off and that was our Saturday.

Sunday was a new day and we spent it quietly trying to make it as uneventful as possible. By sacrament meeting hour I was sufficiently recovered that we went over to church.

Ginny has been very busy. She had a big dinner and swimming party Saturday night for 22 people in her ward, and managed to get organized enough to attend the stake conference meeting at 5:30 p.m. She finished up Rosie's room and moved in all the new matching white furniture. She says Jim keeps going upstairs to take one more look because it looks like a real house—like other people's houses, rather than a collection of hand-me-downs.

Must get to my storage room and straighten up. I have replenished my supply again, but it is all in paper sacks. Dad is coming home at noon today to take one more look at what is happening around here. It is hard on his deliberate conservative nature.

The flood in Idaho has been a real tragedy. Many church members have had their homes and businesses wiped out. I am sending you a clipping from the newspaper.

Love and kisses to all,

Mother

Clark and Kathleen's second child was due within a few weeks. Holly, their first, was just over one year old at this time.

June 15, 1976
Tuesday

Dear Kathy,

It was a shock to write the date and realize that June is half gone. Where does it go?

It is 9 o'clock in the morning and I have already done a day's work. A matter of necessity, as Holly will be showing up any minute and nothing is accomplished after that. Kathleen went to bed yesterday with toxemia and cannot get up even for meals. Clark puts a few gallons of punch by her bed and drops Holly off here while he goes to work for a few hours. He then goes home rather early in the afternoon to get something for Kathleen to eat and frantically paint the walls in Holly's room. She had her cousin out of the U come last week and roll on the first coat of paint over the old wallpaper. The paper buckled and they had to pull it all off, sand the walls, and start over. Then to compound the problem they decided the yellow paint was too yellow. I don't know what they are going to do about that. They were having a big family discussion last night as to whether they should try to get a quart of white and tone it down or buy a whole new gallon of a paler yellow. Such decisions can shatter one's peace and tranquillity.

Kathleen goes to the doctor again on Wednesday, and if the problem is not corrected she will have to go to the hospital for tests to determine whether it is affecting the baby. If so they will have to get the baby born in one way or another. Since she has been seeing the doctor once a week of late and the symptoms did not show up until this week, it could be that they have gotten control soon enough and can get it corrected. Here's hoping.

Ginny had sick children all last week. Everything from asthma to bee stings. She is going to Logan to a writer's seminar Thursday and Friday. Will take three children with her and leave two with me. Oh, how I wish Celia were here. We need her badly, but will look forward to her arrival in July. I hope we can all hold out that long.

One little cheery item—K. came over to dinner Sunday. He noticed we did not have a radar microwave oven and couldn't believe that I was so underprivileged. A new Amana showed up at our door last night. It is so disgustingly lovely. Jane and I have had a ball trying out 40-second scrambled eggs and 1-minute cracked wheat cereal.

More later in the week,

Love to all,

Mother

Kathleen gave birth to a healthy daughter nine days after this letter was written.

June 20, 1976
Sunday

Dear Kathy,

And here we are at the end of another week! Your letter written last Sunday arrived on Thursday. The service is not improving noticeably.

Have the art lessons or scuba diving become a reality? My, how history repeats itself! Funny. I'm so glad it is you and not me. I'm much too tired to try and motivate anyone to make something of his life. Good luck and all my blessings!

Kathleen and Holly moved in with us on Wednesday. She was so lonely lying in bed at home with Holly being farmed out that she took up residency on our kitchen sofa so at least she could be where she could see Holly. She has to stay flat on her back and she gets so miserably uncomfortable that she can hardly stand it. Clark took her home over the weekend, but will bring her back Monday morning after she has been to the hospital for more tests. We are hoping that they will not keep her up there as the cost would be horrendous. She is feeling quite discouraged tonight, as she has gained 5 lbs. in the last two days which means more water-retention and that is what causes a lot of the problem with toxemia. We will know more tomorrow. Holly has just been a little dream. It is as if she fully understands that her mother is sick and that she must cooperate in every way. She does not whine for her mother, but lets me do everything for her. She is such a happy little personality and so cooperative.

Thursday Rosie and Amy arrived and stayed until Saturday night. Amy clung to Rosie like a leech until Rosie was worn to a frazzle. Ginny went to Logan, as I told you, to attend the 2-day seminar on magazine writing. They had exciting speakers with panel discussions by members of *Reader's Digest* and *National Geographic.* Well, we are on our way to another budding career! She was on a fast-talking binge tonight as she gave us the full report of how to become a success overnight.

The kids all came up tonight after church (except, of course, C & K) and brought their weird Father's Day presents. A Tupperware full of home-grown alfalfa sprouts, a plastic bag of home-grown and cleaned radishes, a brown paper sack of green peas from someone's Logan garden. After all, what can you give the man who has everything? Actually, they had planned to give him an electric hand cultivator, but Clark was assigned to make the purchase and of course he is laboring under too many burdens and just flubbed it. Saturday just about did him in, taking care of the house and Holly and Kathleen. He came over after Sunday School today because he heard I had fried 4 chicken breasts for 2 people and he could not think of anything to buy when he did his Saturday shopping except milk and cheese. So we sent the chicken breasts back with him and a few frozen peas.

It is the mission presidents' seminar this week and we will have 20 people here for dinner Thursday night. I don't understand it. We got this place all slicked up for the Windsors not too long ago and here we are again in a frantic mess with a party coming up. They are working on the back deck, with lumber and rubbish all over the backyard. The topsoil delivered more than a week ago is still in the front driveway. The nursery had a sale and there are about 15 cans of various trees and shrubs waiting to be planted. The driveway is in the process of being formed up for the brick and once again it looks like the Hinckleys just moved in. The neighbors look over here and scratch their heads. I think we are out of our element among these manicured yards with husbands and fathers who are home every Saturday. Dad worked half a day on Saturday on Jane's shower. I think Roger can finish it up now, but it will be a real push to get it done before the stork arrives. Jane has been very uncomfortable this past week with leg problems caused by pressure. We are all getting ready to get this baby show on the road. And are we glad that Celia is coming! I only wish she were here now. I am missing your grown-up girls desperately. I need them to help with the dinner Thursday night, as we are setting up tables downstairs and I need some good runners. Also, I will have Holly and possibly Kathleen if she can stay out of the hospital that long. I find I am not so swift at putting on three meals a day anymore.

Completely out of the habit and it is a real chore. Don't laugh. I took it for granted too when I was your age.

It was 96 degrees today. Hot and muggy, if you know what I mean.

By the way, the Father's Day card you sent was a hit. Just the super perfect card.

Dad has gone to bed so I must follow.

Love,

M

P.S. I should keep carbons of these letters so I will know what I have told you and what I just think I have told you. In case I did not tell you—I tore up the check for $7 that you sent home with me. I think it was for lunches we had when Grandma was there.

Tuesday

Kathleen is back on our kitchen sofa and climbing the walls. They will induce labor sometime this week, but have not decided when, so we are all in a holding pattern. You may get a phone call before this letter.

The Hinckleys were preparing to travel to Washington, D.C., for the nation's bicentennial celebration.

June 29, 1976

Dear Kathy and gang,

Lori has come to stay with Kathleen this week and that is a great relief. Ten days with Holly makes me realize that I am not what I used to be. Dad says she is hyperactive, but I say she is just another Clark. Yesterday she dunked her head in the toilet and came up dripping. If she weren't so good-natured and adorable it would be unbearable.

Don't grieve over the cherries and apricots. There were very few cherries and not a single apricot, so enjoy the pineapple and mangoes. We picked what cherries there were yesterday while Dad worked on Jane's shower. With the help of the Pearce monkeys we got enough to put up 21 pints and give everyone a sack full for eating.

Kathleen and Holly went home last Friday and hired a baby-sitter while I got ready for the party with the mission presidents. Because of the wild week we had I did not make any preparation until party day, and it was a mad dash. Mrs. L. came or I never would have made it. We borrowed tables and chairs and seated 23 people downstairs. It worked out very well.

Rosie came up on the bus to the Capitol and did hundreds of little jobs and was a great help, but she was so exhausted she slept until 11 o'clock the next morning.

In Dad's little black book it says that we leave for England August 17th. I hope you are planning to come well before then. Also, I heard him tell someone the other day that we would be going to the Orient again about October. I think the place of the seminar has not been settled, but they are talking of Hong Kong.

Kathleen has gone into the hospital this morning to see if she can deliver this baby. What a poor way to do it. She has been scared stiff ever since she got the word yesterday. It is much better not to know when the zero hour approacheth. Poor Clark is like a walking zombie. Their house is so hot they are sweltering and he was rummaging through everyone's storage last night to see if he could come up with some fans or cast-off air conditioners.

In reading over the schedule for the Washington trip it seems we have a concert at the Kennedy Center and receptions for VIP's, etc., for which I do not have the proper attire. I am going down to Z.C.M.I. this morning to see if anything can be done at this late date with my limited wardrobe. I will probably end up taking a couple of oldies to the cleaners. Dad has five talks to prepare, some of which will go over the Washington TV and radio, so he is under a lot of pressure. Where, oh where, is that peace and rest? But I suppose when and if it ever comes that will be far worse than the pressure.

Love,

M

Marjorie was skilled at helping cousins who lived far apart become close friends. Rosie and Celia were nine and ten years old at this time.

July 1976

Dear Kathy,

Your letter of Sunday arrived today and I felt terrible to think that I had not yet written and that you would be anxious about Celia. I will probably break down and phone you tomorrow or Friday and hope that this letter will arrive by Saturday to fill you in on the details.

Things are working out simply super for Celia. My, how she has matured! She and Rosie have been inseparable and have gotten along beautifully, without a hitch. Never have I seen Celia so talkative. She chats away all day long, as does Rosie, too, and it has been a riot. When they are not talking they are giggling. Right now they are sprawled on the kitchen floor watching the Olympics, and quite frankly it is nice to have them quiet for a moment. They motor back and forth between Pearces and here, having set a goal of not sleeping in the same place for more than two nights in a row.

Saturday Celia stayed here with Gramps and me and Rosie stayed home to help her mother. Saturday afternoon we had a once-in-a-summer thunderstorm. It was a doozie. One inch of rain fell within the first 5 minutes. We went out on our new glass porch and watched the lightning jump over the valley. It hit a transformer across the canyon and a big ball of silver flashed up into the air.

When the storm settled down to a light rain we dropped Celia at Pearces and we went down to the Manti pageant. Got home at 2 a.m. Celia went to Sunday School with Pearces and then Dad and I took Celia and Rosie to church at Brighton, where Dad had to speak. They sat by themselves and got the giggles. We went from there to Clark's ward, where Dad spoke again, and they were thoroughly church saturated.

Monday Dad and I went out to Jane's, where Dad spent all morning working on the plumbing under the sink. Will it ever end? I guess not, until the house is sold to strangers and we get an unlisted telephone. Celia swam all day at the Pearces on Monday and then on Tuesday both Rosie and Celia came back here where they have been working like little troupers. Jane is staying here with the baby for two days while Roger is in Nevada so there is plenty for them to do.

Celia was excited to get your letter, as we all were. Life at your house is unbelievable. That is the first time I ever heard of people crying at a Primary graduation. I thought all children were happy to get out of Primary. It must have changed since my day. I have to speak at one of those things in a couple of Sundays.

Must dash—

Mother

Marjorie saved her children's letters and returned them when the children were older and would recognize their value.

Dear Kathy,

Thank goodness we got the letter from Celia telling us that they had been told about the stork. I don't know if I could have written another letter without mentioning it and I did not want to do so as long as you were holding out. The letter from Celia was a gem and I am returning it complete with envelope for your box of souvenirs. Also, I did find the letters that I had stashed away in my desk drawer. I had looked in the box where they were a dozen times, but they were in a folder labeled "letters" and I had juggled through without reading labels. That's what happens when one is so organized. If they had been junked in the box I would have spotted them long before. Some of the better ones were missing, due to the fact that I sometimes put them in my purse and take them to Ginny or Clark to read. They are checking out their junk corners to see if any of them turn up.

The more we think about the coming event, the better it gets. This will mean that you will have someone making clutter in your house for an additional five years out there in the world wherever you will be in 20 years. Let me tell you that will be a blessing, provided he or she does not turn into a spoiled, demanding, rebellious "only child," which is not likely with the super intelligent parents he will be blessed with.

Saturday I took the Pearce girls to the Fair. They came to the capitol on the bus and piled in the car. I handed Rosie Celia's letter and asked her to read it out loud as we made our way through the North Temple traffic towards the Fairgrounds. At first they didn't understand what the letter was saying, but as they proceeded and it began to dawn on them they acted as if they were stunned. They kept saying things like, "You mean KATHY is having a baby!" As if that were some reversal of Mother Nature and completely out of character. When they finally accepted the fact that it could possibly be true then Laura said, "Well, now they will *have* to move back here, because we will have to take care of that baby." It was one thing that you could *have* the baby, but take care of it—*never!* Dad's comment was, "Do they realize that will be one *more* grandchild for us." Well, it is exciting and we will be hoping and praying that everything will just click along and that these first miserable weeks will pass quickly. Do you have a doctor as yet?

We were invited to Tiffany Attic dinner-theater last week with B. H. and B. S. and wives. The play was "Barefoot in the Park" and was done in super fashion. The acting was unbelievable. Some imported stars and some local but all terrific. After the dinner at the country club with C. G.'s golfing friends and dinner and theater at Tiffany's I am beginning to feel like some sort of society woman.

Dad was in California this weekend and up early this morning to catch a plane to Seattle.

Clark painted their living room white on Saturday. What a mess painting is! In the middle of it they discovered their bishop had been taken to the hospital with pneumonia, so nothing would do but Kathleen stop in the middle of the painting to make a chocolate cake and spaghetti with home-cooked sauce, garlic bread, and the whole works to take over to the family for dinner. They finished up the painting and pushing the furniture back at 1:30 a.m., then got up early Sunday morning to prepare 2½ minute talks which they both had to give. I don't know what it is about this family that they always do things the hard way, but I guess we were not born to be Saturday golfers.

This was going to be a calm Monday, with everyone staying home to do housewifely chores, but Sunday's paper carried a big ad on an auditorium sale on children's clothes, so Kathy has taken her children to a neighbor's and Ginny has dropped Heidi and Amy on my doorstep.

Ginny was gone all day Saturday entertaining all the Relief Society officers and teachers at a luncheon at someone's cabin. It was the first thing to materialize out of all the meetings that they have day after day and was a great success so now she feels comforted.

We had ward conference yesterday and it was the best I have experienced. Instead of classes in Sunday School they had a testimony meeting in which only the youth were invited to participate. It was terrific. I was surprised at the number of solid young people in this ward. It seems to be the high school age group. There is not much here on the college level, but they did themselves proud and all raved about their wonderful bishop. It was interesting to me, as it is a whole unit of our ward that I have no exposure to and did not know of their existence. Almost made me wish I were teaching in Young Women so I would know what is going on in the mainstream of this ward. Almost, but not quite.

Our weather is still balmy and beautiful and I hope to work outside some this week and get the ground ready for the tulip bulbs.

Dad is beginning to worry about his conference talk again. The big question is always what to talk about.

I do hope you will soon have a spurt of energy and be able to get your house finished up. It is a good thing you are adding another bedroom. Maybe you should have made it *two*.

I have a new project, 1 chapter a day from each of the standard works. I have been on it for four days and am only 3 days behind. Better to have tried and failed than never to have tried.

I must get to work,

Love and kisses,

M

Kathy collected Madame Alexander dolls for her children, so Marjorie was always on the lookout for new ones. "Z.C.," short for Z.C.M.I., was one of the premier department stores in town.

November 13, 1976
Saturday

Dear Kathy,

This food storage price list is the only scrap of paper I can find in the hotel in Logan on which to write a letter. We rode up with M. K. and his wife so I have no car. I brought nothing to read as I had hoped to bear down on the last round of my tablecloth, but found I had brought everything but a needle. Before the afternoon is over I will doubtless end up reading the Bible placed here by the Gideons. I've always wondered who read those Bibles. Now I know.

It has been a good week. Beautiful fall weather continues. We have given up on the brick driveway until spring, but did have a cement ridge poured around the driveway, so we can get the pile of topsoil scattered around. If it is still good weather on Monday we should get the yard squared away for winter.

Your letter came on Wednesday this week. Good service. I had just come home from doll shopping in Sugarhouse where I had been with Jane and Ginny scouting the bargains at the outlets. I found "Miss Russia" at the toy store out there and she is adorable. They had a good selection, but am not sure I will get out there again, so may end up keeping "Brazil." She is green and white check and really quite colorful. Z.C. still has nothing.

Have been shopping every day this week. We are trying to get wallpaper and carpet for Mother's kitchen. She sees samples in the store she likes but when she gets them home she doesn't like them. Now I know where I get all these "hard-to-please" genes. Got most of my Christmas done, however. Just Janie and Alan left. If you know of anything Alan would like, send us a message. Otherwise we will get him something he would *not* like.

Love XO

M

Dear Kathy,

This direct dialing system they have to Hawaii is likely to ruin my financial budget permanently. It is such a temptation, and after rationalizing for two or three days I just dial on an impulse. I did come up with a good one this week, however, and that is the fact that we, as a two-member family, spend zero on entertainment, so this is my entertainment money. After all, it does not cost a penny more than a steak dinner for two. Anyway, it was good to get filled in on some of the details which never seem to make their way into letters. I enjoyed every expensive minute of it.

This week has been one big frustration. On Monday we worked ourselves into the ground and did get a lot done outside. We can now sleep while the wind blows. Although there is still much that needs to be done with this yard we have accomplished our goals for this fall.

My winter wardrobe is such that very soon now I am going to have to go into hibernation unless something happens. I have spent the better part of the week trying on every dress and pair of shoes in the Z.C.M.I. Mall.

Ended up with nothing but a pair of shoes, which are going back tomorrow. The dress situation in this town is awful. I tried on seven dresses at Castleton's, forgetting to check the price list. The one that maybe would have done in a pinch was $235. Genuine suede or something. Genuine gold, they should have said. Tried another at Z.C.M.I. which I could have considered, but it was $140 and would have had to have $25 in alterations. I was so desperate by then that I probably would have paid the price if it had not been such an ordinary-looking frock. For that price, one ought to at least feel a little glamorous. I am not exaggerating when I say that I spent 3½ hours Saturday afternoon going through dress racks, pulling dresses over my head and stepping out of them. It isn't that I am fussy. It is just that I want to look respectable.

When I got home from shopping Saturday Jane and Roger were waiting in the driveway to drop Jonathan while they went to Snowbird. They had been trying all day to phone me and just decided they would take a chance on coming up, figuring I would eventually turn up. Jonathan had been eating a lot of pears, and about 20 minutes after his parents left there was an "explosion." I had to strip him down and throw all of his clothes, including his shoes and blanket and my dress, in the washer. All in all, I had a rotten day.

But today has been better. I turned down three invitations to dinner and stayed home to get myself pulled together. Dad just phoned from L.A. to say the plane was late out of Mexico City so he will not be home until 11 p.m., but that is still very good from Mexico.

What Relief Society lesson did you give? Was it the Social Relations? Glad it went well. Tell me more about it.

I suppose you want Heather's name on her scriptures. Confirm this immediately, as they get very busy at the printing counter after Thanksgiving. Do you also want the name on the binder? I am going to get the books tomorrow, as they may get out of stock if I procrastinate, and then I can take them back for name printing when I hear from you.

You had better destroy these letters with Christmas talk in them before some innocent pair of eyes scans the page.

We are going to have Thanksgiving dinner here this year. We have been away for so many Thanksgivings that it is about time I got back in the groove and see if I can still stir up a pumpkin pie. We are going to set up tables downstairs, so the children will not have to be banished to the kitchen table.

I have to talk about women's place in the Church at our stake leadership on December 2nd. Dad gives the welcoming speech at the dinner and then also talks to the men while I talk to the women. Didn't you tell me that you spoke on the same thing in your stake? Better send me your notes.

Love to all,

M

Marjorie spent her sixty-fifth birthday baby-sitting grandchildren. The "Church TV program" she mentions was a national broadcast about families geared to generate interest among a broad range of viewers.

November 23, 1976

Dear Kathy,

I have come over to K.'s to stay with the girls while she goes to decorating class. In her very clean house, and with Holly asleep and Annie being her wonderful little self I have nothing to do, so will write you a note.

Tonight is the much publicized Church TV program. They have carried on such a blitz advertising program here that it could be a real letdown if the program falls short. They are hoping for an avalanche of response with requests for Family Home Evening manuals. Dad did make it a point to advise his non-member "board" friends to be sure and watch. This is a milestone in this kind of proselyting.

Yesterday Auerbachs were offering 10% of every purchase made to the church of one's choice. Since I had experienced such a depressing search for clothes on Saturday I decided to try Auerbachs and bought *three* dresses—bing, bing, bing! I met several people from our ward doing their Christmas shopping and the ward should make a fine-size piece of money.

It was a clever bit of promotion. We have been told that Auerbachs' business has fallen seriously since the Z.C.M.I. Mall. Frankly, it was a relief to shop in an average-size store after trying to find one's way through the miles of aisles in the new Z.C.M.I.

I am 65 years old today. A sobering and melancholy thought. My Medicare forms are filled out and I can ride the buses free. It just seems like a big joke.

Ginny just called to say she has Jonathan while Jane is at a class and that he is being a beast. I will have him all day tomorrow while I am trying to get ready for Thanksgiving. I think I can make it all right if I can keep Dad under control.

Happy Thanksgiving!

Love

M

In the 1970s it was difficult to get Church materials outside of the Wasatch Front, so Marjorie helped with her family's Christmas shopping. Belle Spafford, whom she refers to briefly, had served as general Relief Society president from 1945 to 1974.

December 1, 1976

Dear Kathy,

I have picked up the blue scriptures and they are simply beautiful. I presume that you want her name put on them, but am holding up on that until I hear from you. I also got the zipper covers, but unfortunately they do not make the large double one in blue, which would hold both books. They only come in the singles, which means in order to take all her scriptures along with her she would have to be carrying two packages. However, the black and brown both come in the double size that will hold both Bible and triple. Let me know on this and I can always take the two single blue ones back if you do not want them.

On the dolls—I have the Russian, which is adorable, and also the South American baby, which was the only other one Z.C. had. However, I found at Auerbachs the other day the Portugal doll, which I thought was very cute, so I bought that also. Now you will have to tell me which one you want and I will return the other. When I got home with the Portugal doll she looked strangely familiar and I am wondering if you already have it. Check it out in the book.

Our Thanksgiving was a success. It worked out very well to set up the table downstairs. All I had to cook was the turkey and trimmings. Gin made two pumpkin pies from the leftover Halloween pumpkin. Kathleen brought an ice-cream pumpkin pie which is so absolutely delicious that I am enclosing the recipe. It is one her mother sent her, and the beauty of it is that it can be made a day ahead and frozen and also the leftover pie can be frozen.

We just got Holly back on some kind of a nap schedule and Jonathan goes the no-sleep route. Half-hour in the morning and half-hour in the afternoon and then up at 2 a.m. and 5 a.m. and 7 a.m. for good. The doctor gave him a check-up yesterday and says he is what is called an overachiever and cannot be bothered with sleep.

Must dash—I have to run a couple of errands and try to get some kind of an outline for the leadership meeting tomorrow night. My subject is something about "Women and the Priesthood" or women in the Church today. It is a little foggy, but I think this is the kind of affair where I should be giving a Belle Spafford talk. I'm in trouble.

I had Mother here over the weekend. She is going downhill. Don't know how much longer we can let her stay in her home. If we make it through the winter there, it will be stretching it. She insists that when she has to leave she will go into an apartment, but I am not sure what that would solve, unless she got close enough to me that I could run in every day. In the meantime the painters are painting her kitchen and some new wallpaper will be hung before Christmas.

Love to all—

Dear Kathy,

I will try to remember to stamp this so it will not be a week getting to you. Last week was fairly uneventful. I did a little more chasing around to get Christmas in the bag. It is people like the G.'s that are challenging. I finally ended up getting them a 5-lb. bag of pistachio nuts. Not much of a present, but will have to do.

Thursday was wiped out with the talk I gave Thursday night. Friday Evelyn, Dorene, Joanne, and I went down to Mother's and house-cleaned her kitchen and front rooms. We hired a man to do the walls and windows, so it was not too bad. Mostly it was just sorting out junk and throwing it away. Old broken vases, empty spice cans, and faded artificial flowers. We will try to go again this week and do the bedrooms and bath and then she should be in better condition.

Saturday was a lovely day. It was the monthly temple meeting this weekend, so Dad did not have an assignment. We stayed home all day and did odd jobs. I cleaned the house in the morning and devoted the entire afternoon to the plants. I know that sounds impossible, but it is true. The impatiens had to come out of the front courtyard, at last. Everything needed fertilizing and spraying. Well, you know.

Sunday night we went down to the Church offices to observe the telephone crew as the calls came in from all over the U.S. on the Church program. They had 6,000 calls on Saturday night and 4,500 Sunday. After the rush was over all of the telephone people and their spouses met in the assembly room for a testimony meeting and told of their experiences on the switchboards. It is unbelievable the response that has come. We have concluded that the Mormons were critical of the program (not being the kind of gospel teaching they had expected of a Church program), but the non-members were very impressed. A Lutheran minister called in for enough handouts for his entire congregation. Social workers called in for 40 and 50 copies, and hundreds of children and mothers and fathers from broken homes. So many of the call-ins wanted to know if it would be repeated or if it would be a weekly that they will probably run it again.

D. B. died in his sleep Thursday night. I have never seen Dad more depressed or retrospective. I could not go to the funeral for reasons which I will explain in the next paragraph, but Janie said Dad gave the most super talk she had ever heard in her life.

I could not go to the funeral as I had to have some minor surgery at 10:30 that morning. It seems that I had a very freakish sort of thing. It was a lump on top of my rib cage right under the left breast. Dr. H. has been pondering over it for a couple of months and felt sure that it was breast tissue which was growing outside of my breast. Now, how is that for freakish ailments! Finally concluded that it should be removed in case the tissue itself might be malignant, although he could not feel any lumps that would make it suspect. He sent me to a surgeon about 2 weeks ago and he came up with the same diagnosis—that it felt like nothing but breast tissue, but perhaps should be removed, so I made the appointment for Dec. 2nd, since my Medicare went into play Dec. 1st. Oh, brother! I've really arrived. They just gave me a local and although I could not feel much pain, it traumatized me to be strapped down under those lights with four men in green hovering over my blood pressure and other reflexes and the nurse handing the sponges and clamps. I was trying my best to drop into a black-out sleep and pretend I was somewhere else, but to no avail. Dad came soon after I got back in the room and we came home within an hour, which is the great advantage of not having an anesthetic. They have sent a sample for testing, which will not be back for a couple of days, but the doctor felt that it looked like healthy tissue, so I am not too worried. I was a bit groggy last night from the Demerol they put in my hip, but this morning I am fine except the incision is so sore that I am walking doubled over. We have a Christmas party with the Sunday School tonight, but I guess I will not try to make it.

Well, that's about it. Now that the Christmas shopping and wrapping are done I am going to get busy on Christmas cards. We are only sending overseas this year, but even that is a project, as they all require more than just a signed card.

Love to all,

Mother

Dear Kathy,

Your letter came yesterday and was a great morale booster as I have been pretty much house-bound since the "minor" surgery. Today was a big day, however, I went to the hairdresser and then to the doctor's office, hopefully to have the stitches out, so I could straighten up, but he is not going to take them out for another week. The report from the pathologist was good. They found nothing but breast tissue and fatty tissue, no malignancy of any kind, so I guess the peace of mind has been worth the discomfort.

I am proud of your scrapbook project. That will be a terrific contribution to Christmas and to our faded-out Bicentennial celebrations.

As to Dick and Jane for Christmas, the only list I got from Jane was— Keds, blue or red, size 7½ (she hasn't changed at all), furry, fluffy house-slippers (same size), pink bath mat.

I bought the pink bath mat, but if you are desperate and would like to give her that I can always get the Keds. Let me know. The bath mat was $8.50, believe it or not. You might consider a subscription to *National Geographic*. Some forms I have here list it at $7.50. I am considering sending for this for C and K.

I had 13 seats reserved at the Promised Valley Playhouse tonight for "Christmas Carol." Everyone is going except Jim and Amy and Dad and me. I have been given instructions for everyone to meet Dick at the box office with their money (cash) at 7:50.

The "no snow" winter here has become the topic of the day. Wolfe's have been so badly hurt that the story is everything in their store is going on half-price next week. Castleton's winter clothes and boots are still stacked high. Even the restaurants are complaining because of no ski tourists.

Jane and Roger got a family to play Santa for and we are all helping them. It will really be fun. They have a 2-year-old girl and 4-year-old boy. The 4-year-old boy wants a tricycle and if we can not find one at Deseret Industries we are going to buy a new one.

Dad goes to Mexico again this weekend. He is leaving the office a little early and we are going out to see Aunt Lois and do a couple of errands. Maybe even buy a Christmas tree. We are looking for a 2-footer. Maybe a 3-footer.

Love to all,

M

The Hinckleys had recently returned from a round-the-world tour of missions and Church units, including stops in Asia and Europe.

February 2, 1977
Wednesday

Dear Kathy and everyone,

It is so good to be home I can scarcely make myself go to the cleaners or grocers. Dad asked me if I would like to drive to Phoenix to stake conference February 12th. I declined. And then I remembered what a treat and thrill such an offer held at one time in my life. My, how I have matured.

Somehow Dad made it down to Phoenix last Saturday from where he had to drive 100 miles south to his conference assignment. He left from Denver, as Salt Lake was fogged in, and he had to go without a clean change of clothes or his papers and he had a terrific head cold. But by some small miracle he looked better when he finally got home Sunday night than he looked when he left Denver Saturday morning. He still has a big bass voice and is worried about being in condition for two solemn assemblies this weekend, one in Kansas City and one in St. Louis. When one sees the way the Brethren work compared to the life of the U.S.

presidents described in "Upstairs at the White House," one wonders what we are trying to prove.

Dad could not get over the fact that Eisenhower could spend weekends playing bridge with the entire responsibility of the United States of America on his shoulders. And the fact that President Kennedy found time to swim twice a day was unbelievable. But the wonderful thing was that he said he learned one thing from reading the book and that was that one doesn't have to be a workaholic to be famous. Not that it will make any difference—but it was nice to have him say it.

We found everything well at home. Only lost one plant, which is probably a lower casualty rate than if I had been home.

We had 2 inches of snow yesterday, which is the first since the light skiff we had when you were here. It is very serious and President Kimball has called for a special fast on Sunday for moisture. People are getting panicked again about the "April" food-storage date. Even I am beginning to get a little nervous and think I will put in a few more cans of tomato juice, grapefruit, and orange crystals immediately. There were families in the East who have been snowbound without enough groceries for one week. Not Mormons, I am sure.

I have some February projects, and the first one is to get everything out of my jam-packed closets ready for a trip to Deseret Industries. But with all of this panic going on I am not sure I can do the thorough cleaning out that needs to be done.

I am hoping for a letter from you today. It has been all I could do since getting home to keep from dialing your number, but since the bills this month sent me reeling I am trying to practice discipline.

Love to all,

M

Kathy's husband, Alan, had been transferred from Hawaii to Chicago.

February 13, 1977
Sunday

Dear Kathy and all,

It is a beautiful spring day today, but we cannot enjoy it with good conscience because we need winter so badly. The situation is grim. Maybe come April we will all be glad for our food supply, but none of it is going to be too palatable without water. How much wheat gum can one chew?

We had an "August" type fire on Ensign Downs yesterday, a huge field fire which threatened 3 homes across the street and down a ways. I was coming home from the airport and a visit with Mother when I saw crowds of people, and cars, 4 fire engines, a couple of police cars and smoke billowing all over the place. It was 30 minutes before I could get through. It was an exaggerated rerun of the summer fires we used to have in East Mill Creek. Started by some 8-year-olds playing with matches. When the brush fires start in February the last days must be upon us. You can not believe the panic buying that is going on in this valley. "The Store," which used to be a nice neighborhood store where you could pick up a package of powdered sugar in 5 minutes, has become a teeming nightmare. Even at

9 a.m. it is hardly worth the fight. The merchants are running full-page ads on case lots. Even K-Mart is selling wheat. The grocers are getting rich and all other businesses are suffering because people are spending every cent on food. There is no time of the day or week when you can get waited on at Sterling Nelson's without spending an hour. All this is, of course, hearsay. I go on getting milk from the dairy and an occasional dozen eggs and a little produce from my west-side Safeway's, and looking over my year's supply occasionally and wondering what "vital" item I am missing.

This Chicago move of yours has had us all standing on our heads. It still seems like some kind of a nightmare, but is beginning to look more like a lovely and beautiful dream all the time. The Hawaii experience (except for a few ups-and-downs) turned out to be a never-to-be-forgotten experience, and I am sure the same will be true of Chicago. It is hard on the older girls, because it is always sad to leave friends, but it is also exciting to think that there are people in Chicago whom you do not even know who will someday be near and dear. It is just that Chicago has never been anything to this family except a miserable O'Hare airport with holding patterns and delays and missed flights. However, we did have one lovely experience there when we went on the train to Chicago and then took a bus to Lansing to meet Dad. I think it was after you were married. Jane and I were reminiscing yesterday about how beautiful Michigan Avenue was and how great the museums and how we were all so tired we sat on the ground while Clark walked down to dip his hands in Lake Michigan. This is where Papa Hinckley and Aunt May and Ramona and

Sylvia lived during their mission and Ramona went to the Chicago Art Institute for art study and learned to do beautiful paintings. I have been looking and reading the enclosed map, and it looks like a whole new world is about to become part of our lives. It is quite exciting.

Dad went to Phoenix this weekend for the third week in a row. He will be back at 5 o'clock and wanted me to arrange for some company tonight, but everyone I called is busy. People in this town have so much family that it is hard to get a group of friends together. We did have some Ensign Downs people here last Sunday and it was very enjoyable. There are many people in this ward I would like to know better, but there is so little time to fraternize.

Later:

Dad has arrived home in a super good mood, as he had a gospel conversation with a bearded math professor from Tempe on the plane. He brought home all the citrus fruit he could cram into his bag.

Kathleen has just invited us over for cheese sandwiches, so that's nice. Holly talks not in sentences, but paragraphs. She goes so fast that she stutters and one only catches a word here and there. She also talks with her hands. She is a riot. K. says, "What are we in this family?" and Holly says, "Thweet. Thweet to our mothow." "And what do we do in this family?" "We coopurate."

The letter we got from you this week was a classic again. My, we do enjoy them. I am saving these letters carefully, as they are a terrific journal.

Must go—love to all,

M

February 19, 1977
Saturday

Dear Kathy,

I was certainly glad to get your letter today, as I was home alone and these silent Saturdays are beginning to get to me. I must arrange to have Rosie or someone come up occasionally on a weekend, I guess. Haven't done it of late because it seems like there are always so many things that need to be done there is little time for play. Today I have been painting the bathroom shelves that Dad finally made. There are several winter projects still undone, such as sorting the slides and updating the genealogy books. I did get a grundle of things ready for the D.I., but for the first time in memory, winter wasn't long enough. In fact, it just didn't seem to come at all. Here it is the middle of February and everyone is out working in their yards. We have crocuses blooming in the courtyard. Children are skateboarding and flying kites. Spring has always been so welcome, but this year it is depressing and upsetting. California is already on water rationing and the committees are busy surveying the situation in Utah to see if it can be voluntary at this point or whether it will be mandatory.

Valentine's Day almost got past me completely until I got a call that the Pearces were on their way up with a homemade valentine. I hurriedly scrounged up some homemade of my own and we had a fun time.

Will see what kind of receiving blankets are on the market here. Let's not have green cats on yellow blankets. This baby may be taking a back seat to all the excitement of your daily living, but it certainly deserves an appropriate receiving blanket. Not sure I'll be able to deliver it in person— you know Dad. One minute he is telling me that I will have to meet him at the airport next Sunday night with a clean shirt, as he arrives back from his Idaho conference to take off for Hawaii 45 minutes later. The next thing I hear is that there is no way he can spend 4 days in Honolulu and that it is far from necessary SO—who knows. Maybe we will make it, maybe not, but we will call you one way or another.

Have a busy week coming up. For some reason I can not understand, I have committed myself to a committee in the Cancer Society. I am supposed to be the public education department. I immediately called my friend Z., and if she will do it, maybe I can muddle through.

Hope you are feeling well and not too draggy.

Love,

M

Dear Barneses,

Another week has gone and the sands of time are running out while my projects go undone. I called myself to repentance and stayed up until 1:00 a.m. sorting photographs—mountains of them that have been taken all over the world, most of which are of no particular value, but how can one throw away a perfectly good photograph of a groundbreaking in Taegu! Needless to say, most of them went back in the box, bound in little bundles.

Last Sunday Dad spoke at a 12-stake fireside at BYU. It is unbelievable how 20,000 bodies pack that Marriott Center once a month on a Sunday night after having been in church all day. Before the meeting a reception was held for all of the stake officers and a beautiful buffet was served. They gave me a huge white orchid to hide behind while I sat on the stand with the floodlights penetrating my very thoughts. After the meeting we talked with scores of young people whom we had met all over the world. (I think I was a little slow getting a letter off last week and so maybe I have already reported on this item. Please forgive. I am getting as repetitious as an old woman and at a much too early age.)

Tuesday evening we attended the awards banquet for the *Deseret News* at the Panorama Room. Dad was the principal speaker and gave a very interesting account of some of the problems facing the *Deseret News* this coming year, to keep it in the black while evening newspapers all over the world are slipping. Sometimes I wonder how he can worry about so many things simultaneously.

Friday I went to a Cancer meeting at the center to report on what Z. and I had done as the public education committee. Since Z. has been sick and we had not done anything it didn't take me long to report. We will see what happens when Z. gets on her feet. It isn't the work I mind, but the product we are dealing with.

I have to speak in a Bountiful Relief Society Tuesday on "Sisterhood Around the World" for their birthday luncheon, and this afternoon is the only time I will have to get something organized, so I must sign off and get busy. We have another snowstorm and blizzard in progress. Hope Dad can get into the valley on schedule.

Love to all of you,

Mother

March 24, 1977
Thursday

Dear Kathy,

I checked out the sale racks at the Z.C.M.I. Mall. There is very little left in winter clothes. The spring things are in and at astronomical prices. There is rather a good selection left in pants, but the fit is so tricky that even though the measurements were close to those you gave me, they were not right on and I was wary of buying any, because the prices are too high to gamble with. $13.00 slacks are marked down to eight and nine dollars, but even that seems a lot to pay. In terms of what you are going to pay next fall it might be a bargain.

Purchased the following items:

For Angela:

1 kelly green double-knit culottes	Reg. $11.50	Sale $7.99
1 turtle neck kelly green	Reg. $8.00	Sale $4.99
1 yellow pullover (variegated stripes)	Reg. $11.00	Sale $7.99
1 tan corduroy jacket (lgt. weight)	Reg. $13.00	Sale $1.99
		(super bargain)

(this will give her 4 mix and match pieces)

For Jeff:

    3 polo shirts

Reg. $5.00   Sale $2.99
Reg. $4.60   Sale $2.99
Reg. $5.00   Sale $3.50

For Celia:

    1 pr. pink P.J.'s

Reg. $7.50   Sale $5.99

(This was the only winter sleepwear in the entire mall, except for one in a size 6 for Jeff for $5.00 which were so ugly they would give a child nightmares.)

The staggering total of above articles comes to $38.45. There is no opportunity to bargain hunt for winter clothes, as they are practically non-existent and one is glad to find anything at all, especially if the price is marked down a smidgen.

We are having another snowstorm today, but it melts as soon as it hits the road, as the temperature is so warm.

Love,

M

P.S. One of Ginny's friends who has lived in Chicago told her that the biggest plus for living in Chicago is the tremendous school system in the surrounding suburbs. You could use a few good schools about now.

The Hinckleys had just gotten home after visiting Kathy's family in Chicago and Clark's in Michigan. Marjorie called all her children, then her sister Evelyn, and finally her husband's sister Ruth, looking for someone to talk to.

August 24, 1977
Wednesday morning

Dear Kathy,

There is no justice! When I saw the clean and tidy house which you left and when I think of the clean house you left in Hunakai and then saw the dirty mess you walked into on Ramona Road there is just no justice. I was an absolute basket case last night after saying good-bye to Clark and his little family and then saying good-bye to you and yours and leaving you both in overwhelming situations and then to come home to this echoing silence and finding the notes left by the girls, it was all too much. To top it off, there was no answer at Dudleys or Pearces and a busy signal at Dick's which lasted the entire night. Either they had left the receiver off or their guest was spending an evening at home. In desperation I called Evelyn just to tell someone that I was home, but she had taken Amy and all her little friends to the cabin for the night. I finally got Aunt Ruth and she was a sympathetic listener while I told her about how cruel life is. Then I felt better. Dad kept assuring me that you are young and that somehow, before too long, you would both be settled into a respectable house and have an interesting lifestyle going. I know it is all true, but yesterday it looked bleak.

I kept thinking yesterday that you are right back where you were when you arrived in Hawaii two years ago, and you came out in beautiful style there and you will do the same in Chicago—it is just that the pattern is becoming monotonous. It is like climbing a mountain and as soon as you reach the top you get knocked back down to the bottom to climb it again, but I guess the fun is in climbing and not in arriving.

Dad had thought he would be home this weekend, but he has to go to Baton Rouge, Louisiana, to reorganize a stake.

Love,

M

P. S. Angela: In your note you said "sorry if we got on your nerves sometimes." Now I ask you, how could you get on my nerves? What a thing to say, when you know it was pure joy to have you here. Thanks for coming and for just being you. I love you so much.

Dear everyone,

We are well into another week and thank goodness there is no star-
tling news to report. What we all like around here is peace even to the
point of monotony. However, things are never really dull. Life is so full of
a number of things.

Dad had a good weekend and came home feeling well about our
Central States families. He also had a most pleasant time with the P.'s in
New Jersey, all of which makes me wish that I could have gone with him.
Such a jaunt would have been much more appealing than a trip to Japan
in December. We are still undecided about that one.

However, Dad did suggest that I get Christmas in the bag, just in case,
so I am starting out in another hour to see what I can come up with.
Should be a fun day, but could be more exciting if my bank account were
not so flat.

Saturday and Sunday I was still under the weather somewhat and
although I did go to Sunday School and church I curled up with a book in
good conscience. Read the new biography of President Kimball, put
together over a period of 4 years by his sons, and published by Bookcraft.

You simply can't sell President Kimball short. He is a most remarkable man, and it was an inspiring book. He goes into great detail about the way the Brethren used to work, especially when on tour. So much of what he told was familiar to me that I greatly enjoyed it. I guess those days are gone forever. As we read of some of his mission tours, Dad longed for the good old days, hard as they were.

Sunday night I went out to Ginny's to the girls' piano recital. As usual it was a production, complete with Halloween costumes made by the mother of their piano teacher. It was very much better than the usual kind of piano recital, and the girls thought it "big stuff."

Dad has not been feeling up to par for the last two weeks. I wish I could get him to the doctor, but you know how it is. He has had a wretched pain in the small of his back and a general "washed out" feeling. He has weathered these before and time will take care of it.

Tonight we go to a dinner at the Lion House honoring E. W., and from the looks of the calendar we will be well fed all week.

Must get on with the day,

Love,

M

Dear Barneses and Hinckleys,

It has been a marvelous day. We got up this morning to something like 10 inches of snow. Dad was in Seattle and there was no way I could shovel out, so I settled in for a long winter's nap. I could have found a ride to Sunday School and church, but I knew the minute I began phoning that the neighbors would get over here with their shovels, etc., and I thought it best to just lay low until the sun came out this afternoon. About 3 o'clock it was so beautiful that I put on my boots and began to shovel, but of course, just as I expected, the cars began to stop and men who were not really dressed for such an undertaking thought it their Christian duty to lend a hand. Even so, we did not begin to get enough snow moved to get the cars out. Just a footpath. I called Security to pick Dad up at the airport when he gets in at 8:15 and I settled back in my lovely snug house.

This week has been spent getting all the Christmas shopping and wrapping finished up, and except for Aunt Lois I think all is done. It is a wonderful feeling.

We are getting storm doors and windows to help with the energy crunch. They delivered them on Wednesday, an astronomical cost. We'll have to save energy clear through the millennium to make it a sensible investment. The sad thing was that they made a mistake on the specifications and will have to remake the whole lot of them. But sadder than that is that Dad is determined to install them himself. One a day, he says. That will take us up to about the end of February.

President Kimball just spoke to a capacity crowd of seminary students in the Tabernacle. What a beautiful audience. We watched it on TV and he gave a great talk.

This will be a strange Thanksgiving. We will have Thanksgiving dinner Wednesday night at Dick and Jane's, and Thanksgiving Day will be a typical Hinckley holiday: clean a storage room or change the filters in the furnace, or we might find something to paint if we really look.

Love to all and a very happy Thanksgiving,

Mom

Dear Everyone,

Family home evening has rolled around again, and before Dad calls me in to scripture reading I will dash off a line or two, as this is probably the last opportunity this week to grab a few minutes. As if there is not enough action with getting Christmas on the road and a trip to Japan, it seems that more and more people are getting married in December. I am going to try to get the Christmas decorations up for Thursday, but I can hardly bring myself to unpack the artificial tree purchased at the 1976 after-Christmas sale. I knew it was going to come to this sooner or later, but it is almost more traumatic than turning 65. The only consolation is that it is about the only kind of a tree we could leave up while we run off to Japan. A real live one would only droop and become a fire hazard, so I must take comfort in the fact that it is better than not having a tree at all, or having to decorate one on Christmas Eve after a 10-hour flight.

Must get some cards addressed for overseas tonight, so will sign off. Love to all,

M

In 1980, the Church instituted the consolidated meeting schedule. Relief Society had previously been held on a weekday, so Marjorie and her sisters chose to use that time to work on their family history.

March 22, 1980

Dear Family,

Perhaps a form letter is better than no letter at all. Something must be done about my journal writing and letter writing. The weeks are flying so fast there is little time left to repent. With this in mind I shall see about including the journal and letter writing with one stroke of the pen, or more accurately with one clumsy pounding of the typewriter.

Heather came up from Provo last weekend. On Saturday, she and I went shop-browsing. It has been a long time since I went shopping with one of my girls. I miss it. Such fun we had looking at all the new spring styles and planning what we would buy if we had a million. Hardly bought anything—just some cards and trinkets at the Paper Store.

Sunday, we went to a mission farewell and then back to Capitol Hill Ward to have a second go-around with the new program. I love what it has done to the home schedule, but am not too sure what it has done to the Sunday church experience. No time for leisurely fraternizing or visiting about the goings on in the neighborhood. With no children involved in the local scene I feel isolated from the ward happenings. I am trying to get used to it and know it will improve when our ward is divided next Sunday.

Tuesday night we had dinner with Jimmy Stewart on the 26th floor. He has come to Salt Lake to film a 60-minute Christmas special for Bonneville International Corporation. We sat at a round table with him and President and Sister Kimball and the Monsons. Thank goodness for the Monsons who are show-goers and could talk to him intelligently about many of the movies he has made. He is an old man with grey hair and a hearing aid and a high-pitched voice, but was good company and pleasant in every way. He is thrilled to be starring in the BIC film, as it gives him an opportunity to direct the Tabernacle Choir in one scene. When he saw this in the script he immediately decided to take it on. Also, he says it is the most refreshing telling of the Christmas story he has ever read.

Wednesday after work Dad and I came home by way of the west side Safeway to get some milk. It was six o'clock, the dinner hour. A little boy about 8 years old was ahead of me in the line. He meekly pushed a worn and torn food stamp coupon across the counter and said his mother wanted to know if he could get a can of soup with it. The clerk told him that he could not spend a food coupon that had been torn out of the book and he went away empty-handed. It wasn't until I got out to the car that I realized that perhaps he was actually hungry with no food in the house. It has haunted me ever since. I don't know why I didn't have the presence of mind to take him back in the store and buy him a bag of groceries. Needless to say, I have eaten every meal since with a little more gratitude. Sometimes I forget that everyone does not live so well.

This sounds repetitious, but I have never known Dad to be so busy. He is trying to keep so many balls in the air he does not do justice to anything, and it is frustrating for him. He said last night that he is weary of sitting in meeting after meeting trying to be smarter than he is. At a time when most men retire, he seems to be stretching himself further and further. I told him two nights ago that the sink drain is plugged, but he has not even made reference to the problem as yet.

It is blue skies and sunshine in the valley today. I am not ready for spring. My winter projects are not yet completed.

My sisters and I are using our Relief Society day to work on our genealogy together. They were all here yesterday working on the 4-generation sheets. There are many discrepancies. We will meet again next Wednesday at the library to pursue it further. Great fun!

Finished the Book of Mormon this morning in response to Dad's challenge. No 24-year-old boy could have written it. People wouldn't get into so much trouble if they would read it continuously. What a book!

Love to all,

Mother

Dear ones,

This has been an unusual, uneventful, and much appreciated Sunday. The kind it is a treat to have—just an ordinary Sunday at home. There seem to have been so few over the past several weeks. Dad slept in until 7:30, a small miracle in itself, which means the jet-lag is running its course.

I walked to church. Dad came over for sacrament meeting. We walked home and had roast beef and mashed potatoes. Dad spent the afternoon preparing a talk to give in Dick's stake house at 7 p.m. tonight, a climax to a series of sesquicentennial events in their stake. I read through and marked all the scriptures for next week's Sunday School lesson, a resolution I seldom have time to execute. The only thing that disrupted the tranquillity of the day was that someone picked me up just as I was about to go in the chapel and asked me to come into her Sunday School class and tell the 15-year-olds what it is like to be married to a General Authority.

Yesterday Dad was the speaker at the groundbreaking for the Eldon Tanner building at the Y. This is a building to house business management students. It was quite an elaborate affair with a special erected platform, sound system, and flowers for the ladies. Instead of the usual shovel-turning ceremonies or tractor digging, the first dirt was removed with a "small" stick of dynamite. It turned out to be much more than the slight thud they had expected. Rocks flew through the air, one hitting a young woman about 10 feet from me, and she fell to the ground as if dead. For a few paralyzing moments everyone just stood until it was determined that it was not as serious as had been feared. The ambulance came and took her away, put her arm in a sling, and she turned up in the president's box at the football game a few hours later.

We stayed for the football game. The Y played North Texas from Dallas and they put on a good show with a winning score, so that's our football for the year.

Tomorrow, if it doesn't rain, we will have the big fall cleanup in the yard. What needs doing will take much more than one day, but that is all it will get. We at least need to get a few new tulip bulbs in the ground, and then what comes will come.

I have decided that autumn leaves look simply beautiful on the ground, and if we can rake a few off the lawn I am not going to worry about the rest. Our sidewalk is covered—the neighbor children have been having a great time in them.

Tuesday morning

Monday I worked out in the yard and after three weeks of sitting in meetings and riding airplanes and buses I find I am in terrible shape. I hurt from head to toe last night. This being Veteran's Day, Dad is home and he has worked outside all morning and is now glued to the kitchen sofa.

While Dad was doing his yard work this morning I went shopping with Ginny. This is the ultimate in recreation for me. We went to Pier 1 to buy baskets for Christmas projects. Also went to Utah Woolen Mills and simply drooled over the gorgeous merchandise. Bought nothing. She was looking for sweaters for the girls, but they do not carry anything but adult sizes.

I think Dad is off the sofa now, so we are going to buy a lawn rake so I can get my outdoor chores finished. Rain and snow predicted for tonight, so we must get moving.

Tonight Dad speaks at the Mayflower Society at the Panorama Room. He spent most of yesterday preparing a talk. He is sick, sick, sick of grinding out words.

Love to all,

Mom

Dear ones,

It is well into the new year and I scarcely have Christmas out of my system yet, although I hope it is all packed away and out of sight for another year. The very worst part is putting it all away—not just the work, but the melancholy of it.

The sky is still grey in the valley. It has been a long time since we saw the sun. It could be depressing, but actually it is very cozy and puts one in the mood for in-the-house projects.

Christmas this year was very quiet for us. Christmas Eve at Ginny's with the children was just what a Christmas Eve should be. Magic. Christmas morning we went over to Dick's and saw four excited children throwing papers every which way. They had a good Christmas, but not an expensive one.

From Dick's we drove out to Ginny's. Santa left them a darkroom set-up for developing film. Much to Santa's surprise, they were more than excited. They even got a second-hand enlarger which was not working too well the last I heard.

At noon Christmas day we were back home. Made a fire in the

fireplace and spent the rest of the day reading. I read "The Best Christmas Pageant Ever" from the Michigan Hinckleys, and Truman Capote's "Thanksgiving Visitor" and "A Christmas Memory," all of them delightful. We did not go anyplace the rest of the day and no one came. I kept wondering how come I was so happy and content instead of being sad and lonely. It was so incredibly wonderful to just sit in a rocking chair and read without having a guilty conscience.

The night after, we had our Christmas dinner with ham and all the Christmas goodies everyone had sent. The children all sat in the kitchen except the two littlest ones, James and Jodi, who sat in the dining room with parents. This way we only had one glass of milk spilled on the good carpet. It was a fun night.

During the holidays there were various other parties to which I wore my new black velvet dress which Dad gave me for Christmas.

On Tuesday night we both spoke at the Missionary Training Center to 1900 missionaries. The very sight of them was overwhelming. If each one brings in one convert, the result will be mind-boggling. What a church!

Last weekend the U.S. Ambassador from mainland China was here from Washington at the invitation of the Church. Friday he was given the grand tour of BYU, ending with a dinner for about 15 at the president's home. I thought no one could equal Dallin Oaks as a charming host, but he has met his match in Jeff Holland.

After the dinner a handful of the Young Ambassadors with whom we toured China last May entertained with some of the songs from their tour. To see those beautiful kids again and hear those songs which we came to love was a thrill. Many of the songs they sang were in Mandarin and they also gave their memorized speeches about brotherhood in Mandarin. The ambassador was completely captivated. He could scarcely believe his ears. No place but BYU with its Chinese-speaking returned missionaries could this happen.

Saturday night he was hosted at Little America Hotel by the man who owns all the Little America hotels, plus Sun Valley, plus Sinclair Oil and many other enterprises—very bright and very knowledgeable. This was an experience for us as well as the ambassador. There were about 24 people at the dinner and I was asked to give the prayer and blessing on the food. (Frightening.) Mr. Ambassador reiterated afterward that he was an atheist and a Marxist, but there was no reason we couldn't live together in peace.

Love,

M

Letters from

a World

Traveler

*A*s Marjorie's children began to be older and more self-sufficient, she was able to accompany her husband on more of his overseas assignments. She wrote marvelous letters about her travels, filled with details of the places they visited and the happenings there. Her descriptions of Church meetings, shopping trips, and airplane and train rides painted vivid pictures for the family members back home. Her love for the missionaries and her unfailing enthusiasm for the experiences she was having in every country come through clearly. What fun it would have been to travel with her! Through these letters, which span the years from 1958 to 1980, we almost feel as if we have done just that.

From left: President Harold B. Lee, Freda Lee, Marjorie Hinckley, Elder Gordon B. Hinckley

Marjorie wrote not only to her children and grandchildren when she was traveling, but to her parents. The Hinckleys were in England at this time for the dedication of the London Temple.

England
August 31, 1958
Saturday morning

Dear Mother and Daddy,

This is truly a beautiful and wonderful place to be. As you know, the temple is situated on an old English estate. We are staying on the second floor of the old mansion house which the Church has restored and renovated. Our bedroom window looks out across a wide lawn to the temple. It is only 10 a.m., but the people are already streaming through the building. They come in cars, public buses, chartered buses, bicycles, motor bikes, and motorcycles at the rate of about 3,000 a day. It is simply amazing because there has been little advertising except by word of mouth and this is such an out-of-the-way place. The temple is in Surrey county; 2 miles to the south is Sussex county where we go on the bus to eat every morning and evening.

This must surely be the most beautiful part of England. The manufacturing towns are up north, but down here is nothing but the beautiful

English meadows and countryside that the poets have written about. The most enjoyable times we have are in the evening when we join the missionaries on the front steps of the temple to meet the people as they come out and answer their questions. We talked with a young couple last night who are engaged and were just intrigued with the idea of eternal marriage.

We had a beautiful moonlit night last night. As I looked up at that beautiful spire with the floodlights on it and the crowds of people all curious and interested to know what Mormonism is all about, I thought of our grandparents in Sussex county and in London 1½ hours to the north and wondered what they would think if they could look upon this scene. There were some onlookers who wondered why I was weeping.

Our missionaries here are doing a magnificent job. They are so sweet and gentle with the crowds and are able to answer their questions with an intelligence that astounds me.

We plan to go up north on the train to Preston, Gordon's first field of labor, sometime next week. Also plan one day at the fair in Brussels. This is marvelous as long as I can keep my mind off home and the kids.

Love,

M

February 14, 1962
Wednesday evening

Dear family,

We have just arrived in Hong Kong after a dizzy 2½ days in Manila. What a place! No words could describe it.

Manila is a big, noisy, dirty, smelly city of 2 million people. There are no public schools so there are hundreds of children on the streets all the time. The traffic is so wild that unless you can find a street with a semaphore you can't cross on foot without the aid of a traffic cop to stop the cars.

Thursday morning

A large aircraft carrier came into Hong Kong yesterday with 90 Mormon boys aboard, so Dad and the mission president went aboard to hold a priesthood meeting with them. The ship was so large it could not come into the harbor, so it was about a 45-minute ride out to sea. Dad said there were some wonderful boys aboard and he thoroughly enjoyed it. While they were gone the president's wife took me on the "Star Ferry" to the island part of Hong Kong and then on a trolley car to the top to the hill overlooking the harbor. It was a fantastic ride. It makes the hills of San Francisco seem like nothing. The view was fantastic.

Friday 6 p.m.

I seem to have an awful time to write letters. There is never any time. Yesterday Dad had some business in town so I went with him and we looked around in a few shops. I tried on a beautiful mink jacket worth about $800 or $900 at Z.C.M.I. Dad bargained with the man until he came down to $200, but since I had just paid $85 for a new coat the week before leaving home we did not buy it. But it was fun anyway. Dad is having a summer suit made so that he will have it to wear in Hawaii.

Thursday at 5 p.m. we started a testimony meeting with all the elders in this area (78). It lasted for 4 hours and then went from 7 a.m. this morning until 2:15 p.m. at which time we went en masse to a hotel and had Chinese food. I then tried to find a beauty parlor where I could have my hair shampooed, but they are still closed from the Chinese New Year holiday. There is a reception at the mission home which starts in 30 minutes. This is for all members and their friends and will last for the entire evening so will have to end tomorrow. Dad is holding a workshop and interviewing missionaries. I hope to see a little of the town.

On Monday we will go to Formosa for a week and I will not write from there as mail is slow to get out, but will try to send another note from Tokyo where we should be on February 19th.

Hope you are all well and happy.

Mother

Dear Kathy and Alan and Heather,

We have just concluded a 7-hour testimony meeting and Dad has just started a workshop. Since I have heard it, I'll make use of the time by writing you. I feel terrible that I haven't written more. I've only written the kids twice and Dick twice and I think this is only the second time to you. Dad did not bring his tape recorder and I have tried to keep a diary and a record, which is about all I can manage, and I have to do that while riding trains and planes. The only trouble is that these jets are so fast the rides are only one or one and a half hours and we just get all the paper filled out and eat the refreshments and it's time to get off.

All last week we were in Taiwan and I loved every minute of it. We started at the north end in the capital of Taipei and took a 6-hour train ride to the southern tip for meetings there. The countryside was so fascinating I didn't get any notes written. Except for a little Western style in the dress of young people there is nothing which would remind one of home. Rice paddies, oxen and geese in the streets, newsstands on every corner, and shops, shops, shops, shops, big baskets filled with huge tangerines for 30 cents a basket.

I really loved the people in Taiwan. We have wonderful service people there. The Chinese members I really liked, too. Some of them could talk a little pidgin English and they were really fun. I went to a Chinese Relief Society in Taipei. It was cold and clammy—concrete floor, no drapes, about as cheerful as a prison cell—but those sweet service wives were there even though they couldn't understand a word.

On the way back from the south we took a side trip to Sun Moon Lake. We got off the train at 6 p.m. and piled into a taxi. By the time we got into the mountains it was dark and a heavy fog had settled. Sister T. and I were nearly hysterical by the time we reached the lake. It was a narrow winding road with the mountain on one side and a deep drop on the other and visibility about 5 feet. The next morning the fog had lifted and the lake was beautiful. The hotel on the side of the mountain overlooking it was a fabulous place. We rented a small boat with an outboard motor and a Chinese sailor and started for an island to see an aborigine village. About halfway out we could see the fog rolling in and by the time we reached the island, visibility again was about 5 feet. We tried to get the Chinese boy to take us back without going ashore because a stiff breeze had come with the fog, but he said the motor was sounding strange, so he pulled up to the pier and we got out. We walked through the village for about 45 minutes, which was mostly shops for tourist attractions, but the people were interesting and apparently we were, too, the way they stared at us. It was bitter cold, and though most of the children had some sort of a little jacket they were all bare footed. When we went back to the pier our boat was still dismantled but we got a ride back in a larger one, jammed with about 25 Chinese where there was room for about 12. The wind was still blowing and the fog thick. We really weren't in any danger, but you know me!

One hour later

Sister A. and I finally left the meeting, as she had a dentist appointment. She brought me back to the hotel so I could get cleaned up a little for the evening meeting. What a luxury! Usually we go to the night meetings without even combing our hair.

As I was saying, the ride back down the mountain from Sun Moon Lake was worth the whole trip, as we got out of the fog and went through the many picturesque little Chinese villages. They must not have changed much since 1492. It was really interesting.

Back in Taipei on Friday night we went to dinner with the servicemen's coordinator. American food—the first we had eaten on Taiwan. But I enjoyed the Chinese food tremendously. Everyone was amazed that I didn't get sick, but I always did get along well with food. I'll be disappointed if I don't lose weight on this trip, however, because we are lucky if we get two meals a day. We usually settle for one. Yesterday we didn't get anything at all until 8 p.m. and all they served on the plane was a cake with a teaspoon of artificial cream.

Saturday in Taipei Dad held workshops and interviews all during the day, so Sister T. and I decided we would see the town. We were just wondering how to go about it when K. C. and her husband walked into the hotel lobby and said they had come to show us around. They had an old car which they had wired together, and we had a wonderful time with them. We went to the gift shop where Dad bought the Chinese paintings to see if they had something a little larger, but they did not have anything I liked. They then took us up into the hills and we hiked down a little narrow path to some rice paddies which were terraced on the side of the mountains. We saw some Chinese huts at close range. It reminded me of the China described in *The Good Earth*.

Sunday was a full day. We started with a servicemen's conference at 8 a.m. Then a conference with all the Chinese members at 10 a.m. Said good-bye to Taiwan and all our friends, many of whom came to the plane. Flew to Okinawa and got there 30 minutes late for a meeting with the Japanese members at 7:30 p.m. and then rushed across the island for a servicemen's conference at 8:30 p.m. Monday morning we started the routine all over again with a testimony meeting with the elders. Since there were only 8 of them on the island we were through at 10:30 a.m., so we went with some of the members to visit the factory where they claim to make the best lacquer ware in the world. It could hardly be called a factory. It was just an oversized carpenter shop with Japanese sitting on the floor with their legs crossed carving each piece by hand and then painting and polishing and painting and polishing and painting. They had everything from soup bowls to triple dressers. I surely got a new appreciation of lacquer ware. Would like to have had a set of soup bowls but they cost $15 a dozen.

My idea of a good time would be to have a purse full of money and go shopping in this part of the world with you and Ginny. Silk for $2 a yard. Dressmakers about 3 to a block who will make a dress to order for $1.25 to $2.50. No patterns required. Just have to show them a picture or tell them what you want. I paid 60 cents for a shampoo and set at the hotel in Taipei, and thought that was good, but the servicemen's wives say they can get the same on the outskirts for 25 cents. Full-time maid service for $10 a month. This includes washing, ironing, cleaning, baby-sitting, and some help with the cooking. This is all in Taiwan. Things are more expensive here in Japan. However, I bought some silk in Hong Kong and since we are going to be in Tokyo for a week I am going to try to get it made up, as I will need it when I get to Hawaii. The few clothes I brought have taken a beating.

Well, Dad has arrived at the hotel to partake of a shave before the meetings tonight. We are really living in style compared to the schedule we kept in Taiwan. Dad has a cold and his voice is very husky. The schools in Tokyo are closed because of an epidemic of Asian flu. A lot of people are wearing masks, but these Mormons pay no attention.

How is our little doll? I can hardly bear to look at the children here, it makes me so homesick for her. Please don't let her forget us.

Well, Dad is calling, so will have to obey. I will try to write once again before we leave Tokyo. We are going over to Korea next week and I am really looking forward to that.

I have never done so much preaching in my life. The English gatherings aren't too bad but the ones with translators are beastly, especially since we came to Japan. In China I had mostly young Chinese girls translating for me and they were more frightened than I. Dad does a wonderful job—especially with the missionaries. He has been sharp with the wit and they really enjoy him. It is amazing how he can remember their names and faces.

I've enjoyed most of all the testimony meetings. It becomes apparent in a very few minutes after those meetings start whether or not they are dedicated and devoted missionaries. There certainly are all kinds, but most of them are just tremendous.

Give Heather-B a hug. I just get starved for her. Love to all of you. We hope and pray that all is well with you.

Love,

Mother

Bessie was a widow who lived next door to the Hinckleys in Salt Lake. She was like a grand-mother to the children, and she helped keep an eye on them so that Marjorie felt more com-fortable in her travels.

March 1, 1962
Thursday

Dear Kathy, Alan and Heather B.,

I am confining myself to the hotel today, as it is raining (the first we have had in a whole month of travel) and I have a bit of a cold. Have busied myself with washing, rearranging the things we have collected along the way, and letter writing. Have just finished 7 pages to the kids. Gin wrote us one page the week after we left, which we received in Hong Kong, and we haven't had another scratch from home. The only thing that has saved me is one note from Mother last week and a note from Bessie to assure me that everything is fine at home. I really can't complain, though, because I have been a bit negligent myself. Have had a hard time to write with these meetings going on night and day. We are now through with the meetings in Japan. The men have been busy getting a building program under way, so this has given me some free time in Tokyo.

Will start back with last Saturday. We went down to Osaka, a little town of 5 million people, to meet with the saints and missionaries. Saturday afternoon while Dad was interviewing, I went tracting with 2 elders. What an experience! At the first couple of houses I wanted to run and hide, but after that it got quite interesting. We were in quite a good neighborhood where all the homes had walls around them. The biggest problem was opening the gates. When you get through the gates and past the dogs you don't bother with such formalities as knocking—you just open the doors and walk into the entrance hall and call to see if anyone is home. Either the maid or the lady of the house comes and drops on her knees and remains kneeling during the entire conversation. The first few gave us the "too busy" brush off. One lady invited us to sit on the step in the entrance hall and they gave her the 5-minute door approach. She seemed interested at first, but then cooled. We went upstairs in an apartment house and were trying to get a conversation going with a grandma in a doorway when the landlady came flying up the stairs with all the kids in the apartment at her heels to tell us that we had no business in there without permission. The elders explained what we were doing and she calmed down and took a tract. Between houses the elders made me hand out tracts to all the passersby and repeat a Japanese phrase which says, "Please read this, please." I just about choked on it the first time, but I will say for these Japanese—they are very polite. They took the tracts and said "Thank you." The elders got an appointment to go back to one place on the following Tuesday night. I would surely like to have been there to go back with them. It was a fabulous house with beautiful gardens and a wall about like the one on Temple Square. I've never seen so many beautiful walls—blocks and blocks of them. Beautiful rock walls— bamboo walls with mud and gorgeous oriental plants growing on them.

On the way home from tracting we went through a huge outdoor market. You couldn't see the end in any direction—one maze of food and merchandise—nylons and whale meat, bolts of silk, stacks of china, baskets, noodles, fish. We bought some sweet potatoes they were cooking in deep fat. They rolled them in newspaper and we took them back to the branch hall, where everyone was clamoring for a taste. They were delicious.

Sunday was a rough day. Meetings started at 8 a.m. Dad talked to the priesthood (from 5 districts). I talked to the Relief Society. Some had been travelling since 5 a.m. to get there. The translator I had could speak beautiful Japanese, but she had trouble understanding my English. The general session of the conference for all Japanese members, missionaries, friends, and investigators started at 10 a.m. We spoke, and then we had to leave before the meeting was over to get a plane for Hokkaido on the North Island (90 miles) for an evening meeting. We had a 30-minute stopover in Tokyo. R. G. came down to the plane with a lunch in a huge brown paper sack (which we didn't eat until late Monday afternoon) and two letters from home, one from Bessie and the other from you. I sat me right down in the middle of 10,000 people and laughed and laughed. As soon as we got settled back on the plane I handed your letter to Dad, and when he began to read, I thought he was going to burst his safety belt. It really struck him funny.

Well, we arrived in Hokkaido Sunday night after two plane rides and a long bus ride. I was ready for bed, but we all piled into a small taxi and went out to the branch hall, only to find it in darkness. They expected such a large crowd that they rented a hall downtown and forgot to tell us.

After driving around for a while and making inquiries we arrived 30 minutes late. There were about 200 saints and missionaries, and so without washing our faces or combing our hair we made some more speeches, and then shook hands with everyone, and then went to the hotel only to find that they were filled. We had to stay in a Japanese inn, which proved to be delightful. It was dripping with atmosphere. They fixed us a real Japanese supper and we sat on the floor in a cubicle of a room while the Japanese maid fluttered around us like a bird to see that we ate everything. The only thing I could recognize was the rice and boiled oysters. I ate everything, however, except the caviar (fish eggs) and the raw fish.

Monday morning we met with the missionaries and left about 3 in the afternoon to return to Tokyo. Hokkaido reminds me of the way I imagine Alaska to be. There were snow banks 5 and 6 feet on each side of the road. The streets are narrow. Everyone dresses in fur boots, mittens, and caps. Hardly any of the missionaries up there know a thimble full of Japanese. There are 2 sisters there—one has been there 5 months, the other 9 months. They can just barely say enough Japanese to get on and off the buses. They can read the first lessons to their investigators, but they do not understand a word they are reading. They have to dress in everything they own when they go out tracting, and even then it is a fight to keep from getting frostbite on their toes. I really felt sorry for those 2 girls.

There was a young boy from Salt Lake there who didn't look a day over 17. He had been there 3 weeks and had the gom-boo so badly he looked transparent. They had taken him to the hospital on Saturday to get a shot and some medicine, as he was afraid he wasn't going to be able to make it to

Hokkaido for the conference. I could have cried every time I looked at him. Even Dad felt depressed. When we got on the plane to return to Tokyo he said he felt like we were running off and leaving those kids to the wolves. It's rough up there. This mission is much too big and the missionaries get too little attention. It is 1600 miles from the south to the north end.

The ride back to Tokyo was anything but pleasant. They ran into a "little turbulence" and had to change course. The Japan Airlines serves only one menu—it consists of 3 dry sandwiches and a cup of sickly sweet jello. It was late when we got back to the hotel Monday night and I felt really tired—for the first time.

Tuesday morning I spent at the hotel, which isn't too hard to do as it is like a small city. The basement is one arcade after another of beautiful shops—furs, pearls, book shops, gift shops, silk shops, beauty shops, restaurants, flower shops, etc., etc. Sister A. picked me up at noon and took me out to the mission home where I had an appointment for a fitting with a dressmaker. Perhaps I told you that I bought a piece of silk in Hong Kong. The material is pretty, but it looks just like a balloon on me. I'll have to remodel it when I get home, but I will need it in Hawaii. The few clothes I brought with me have taken a terrible beating.

Wednesday we went to a department store—the finest in Tokyo. We spent 3 hours there. It sort of makes ZCMI look pitiful! We stayed 1 hour in the food department. Never have I seen such strange-looking food so beautifully displayed. One floor is devoted to foreign imports. In the French department they have samples of clothes by a particular French designer and you pick out what you want and they take your measurements and make it. Never have I seen such beautifully styled clothes, outside of Christian Dior in Paris. On March 4th it is Girls' Day (like Mother's Day). They were displaying Japanese doll houses for little girls, complete with dolls, $100 to $1000. The most elegant little things you have ever seen. We ate lunch in the store, which was an experience in and of itself. They were serving about 1,000 people at once, and there was no such thing as getting a fork or spoon, so I had to manage with the chopsticks. I made it to the bitter end, but found I had an audience. But I am getting used to that now.

This is a marvelous part of the world—strange beyond words. You must plan to come someday. It all seems like a wild dream to me.

There is surely a lot of work that needs to be done here to strengthen the Church. The integration of new members is sadly neglected. Teaching in the organizations needs improvement. Dad could spend his full time here to advantage, just going from mission to mission and district to district, but I'm not about to mention it.

Send us another letter as soon as you can. We surely enjoyed the last one. Heather's love of animals doesn't sound like us! Must be the Barnes in her. What I wouldn't give to get hold of her for just 5 minutes!

Love,

Mother

Dear Folks,

We arrived in Seoul, Korea, 11 a.m. Monday and have stayed through Thursday morning. It is Thanksgiving, but no celebrating in these parts. It was a bright sunny day when we arrived, clear and cold, but no snow. As we piled out of the station wagon at the home, 40 elders lined the stone walk on both sides, singing, "Come, Come Ye Saints." I had to pretend it wasn't happening or I would have been bawling all over the place. Some of the elders were crying as it was. We immediately gathered around the stove in the dining hall and started a meeting with the sacrament and then had testimonies for 4 hours. Gordon and I then spoke, as did the member of the building committee who is travelling with us.

Two of the elders are local Korean boys. They are the first to serve full-time missions and are being supported by the servicemen here. They bore beautiful testimonies in English; all the elders, as well as us, were crying. They seemed to represent everything that the elders here work so hard to bring about. There is always something so special about these meetings in Korea. I told the elders I had lost all interest in heaven. This is plenty good enough for me. After the meeting they set up a long table in the dining room and had a delicious meal with all kinds of groceries and goodies from the P.X. We then drove out to the military base and had a meeting with the servicemen. All the elders came to the meeting, so there were well over a hundred.

Tuesday morning we were awakened by the singing of the elders at 6:00. We hurriedly got dressed and went for an early morning walk around the beautiful grounds, just as the sun was coming up. Then said good-bye to all the elders who were catching trains back to their various areas. This left only 11 who live at the mission home and work in Seoul. The rest of the day the men had business, so I had a day off. Went down to the silk market and gift shops and had a wonderful time.

Wednesday morning we rode a plane down to Taegu in central Korea. We went out to inspect the branch hall and then to the home of Brother and Sister H. for lunch. He is a full colonel in the U.S. Army and has a nice home on the base. We had a delightful visit with them and caught the 4 P.M. plane back to Seoul. Got to the mission home late. Had some peanut butter sandwiches, visited awhile with the elders, and went to bed very tired. Forgot to say that we went out to visit a Korean orphanage in Taegu, probably the best one in Korea, and it was very impressive. They have about 12 individual homes on the compound. One house mother takes 9 children of various ages in one home and raises them as her own children until they are ready to go out on their own. This is a paradise compared with other orphanages here, as they are richly endowed by an international organization. Many orphanages here are so bad the children try to escape, as they would rather live on the streets.

We are now flying from Seoul to Osaka, Japan, where we will hold a meeting with the elders there at 3 p.m. in the branch hall. This will probably go late into the evening, as Gordon is interviewing all of them this trip and this takes a lot of time. There should be about 40 elders in Osaka. We will stay at the hotel there tonight. We just had our Thanksgiving dinner of cold fried chicken, which we did not eat, a bun and a piece of cold lunch meat, and a big red apple which was delicious. Hope you are both well and that you have a nice Thanksgiving without working too hard.

Love,

Marjorie

The year before this letter was written, the Hinckleys had "mortgaged the chicken coop," as Elder Hinckley put it, and taken their youngest daughter, Jane, nine years old, with them to the Far East.

December 1, 1964

Dear Folks,

We are flying a small puddle-jumper from the south part of Taiwan back up to Taipei, the capital city in the north. Our party completely fills the plane—two building supervisors, two elders, the Chinese architect, the mission president, and the pilot. It is a little bumpy for writing.

It was beautiful in the south. Sunshine with temperature around 75 degrees. Flowers in bloom, especially the poinsettias. They are harvesting the rice and sugar cane. The narrow streets are jammed with water buffalo, bicycles, chickens, children, and honking taxis. We came down yesterday by plane, train, and taxi, stopping at 2 places to meet the elders long enough for interviews, but not meetings.

Had a meeting with 15 elders this morning, after which Gordon interviewed each and I visited with them.

Later in the day

Arrived back in Taipei this afternoon. Have had my hair shampooed and set for 90 cents and we are getting ready now to go to dinner with a prominent attorney, Dr. F. He sent a printed invitation to our hotel room. He is not a member. The Grand Hotel where we are staying in Taipei is Chinese and the most grandiose hotel I've ever set foot in. President Q. had 4 dozen roses sent to our room. They are very beautiful and very cheap. I'm enjoying the Chinese food, as usual, but I've had a little bout of goofy wobbles this time. I haven't missed any meetings or appointments, however, so can't complain. Many of the elders who were here a year ago have asked about Jane and expressed their disappointment that she did not come this time.

We have kept a rugged schedule this time, as we have tried to meet with the Saints, as well as the missionaries and servicemen, plus all the business with the buildings. They have a building almost completed in Taipei, the one we went to the groundbreaking for when Jane was here. It is one of the most attractive buildings in the church—the first in China. The Saints are thrilled with it, but it is so large they will rattle around in it except for district conference.

The number-one problem in Taiwan is keeping the young people active. They have practically no time for church if they are in high school or universities, as the competition in the schools is so terrific they even go to classes on Sunday. If they get anything below 90% on any test they are automatically dropped. They are under terrible pressure.

Hope you are well.

Love,

Marjorie

October 17, 1966
Monday evening

Dear girls,

Last Friday was pure delight. We took a day off and went to Nikko, Japan. Ate breakfast in the mission home at 5:30 a.m. I then walked about 4 blocks through the quiet streets to the subway. We got in the wrong train and had to run like mad to get in the right one. At that early hour of the morning we had the subway station and cars practically to ourselves. A unique experience. At the end of the subway line we boarded a very modern, clean train and rode two hours through the beautiful countryside of Japan up into the mountains. Nikko is a resort town way up in the mountains. I thought I had seen beautiful autumns, but I've never seen anything to compare with that. We hired two taxis and went way up into the mountains to look at the beautiful lakes, waterfalls, and temples. We had a delicious Japanese dinner at a Japanese inn and tramped around until 4 o'clock in the afternoon and returned to Tokyo in time to get swallowed up in the 6 o'clock subway traffic. That, too, was an experience. It was the first time I have seen anything in Japan outside of the big mad cities and it gave me an entirely different feeling about Japan. It was simply beautiful!

Saturday was a day I would like to forget. We left Tokyo at 8:30 in the morning to fly to Okinawa, but we made the mistake of stopping over at Osaka to see some property. We walked around in the building where Jane slept so many hours in the futon bed and then fought that terrible traffic back to the airport to continue on to Okinawa. They calmly informed us that the plane would be 5 hrs. late. So we sat around that miserable, cold, smoke-filled, jam-packed, dirty station with all the other ugly Americans and finally at 9:30 at night they flew us back to Tokyo. Another long wait in a not-so-bad airport and then a 2-hour ride to Okinawa, arriving at 1:20 in the morning. There were still some faithful souls waiting, but we had missed our chance to meet with the elders and servicemen. Sunday morning Dad got up and went up north on the island to see some property, interviewed 16 missionaries, and was ready for the dedication at 9 a.m. About 350 people came. They gave us beautiful leis of ginger flowers, which smelled so beautiful, but Dad sneezed all through the meeting. We shook hands with the entire congregation after the meeting and visited with many of the servicemen. Some were on a weekend pass from Vietnam. Had lunch at the Officers Club with one of the servicemen and his wife and 5 children and then went to the airport to take off to Taiwan for a 5 o'clock dedication. The plane was 2 hours late so we stood around the airport saying our good-byes over and over to about 30 people who stayed until the bitter end. We arrived in Taipei to get the crushing news that there was nothing available at the Grand Hotel, which is one of the most exciting things about Taiwan. Grand Hotel is booked through

January. Dedicated the building—this is the one they broke ground for when Jane was here. The meeting was long. We used earphones with someone translating. It was tedious. Got back to the hotel at 9:30. Had some soup and papaya in the dining room and went to bed.

This morning we went back to the chapel for a 3½ hour testimony meeting. Then Dad began the ongoing task of interviewing 54 missionaries. The mission president's wife and I visited with the lady missionaries for a couple of hours, then got a couple of them to take us downtown. We went to Haggle Row, where I bought some bamboo plates for patio serving. Dad didn't get back from interviewing until 7 and we went to the dining room for a steak. We had eaten nothing but fruit all day. Dad has had the gom-boo all the way since Korea, but is feeling some better tonight. We took a little walk up the street for exercise, but the smell of the food stands along the sidewalk was turning Dad green so we have come back to fall in bed. We are taking a plane early in the morning for the south end of Taiwan.

Love,

M

Samtani, mentioned in the first paragraph of this letter, was an East Indian who had a large tailoring business in Hong Kong. The wish Marjorie expressed at the end of the letter to walk the streets of Hong Kong with her children was fulfilled in celebration of the Hinckleys' fiftieth wedding anniversary, when the children and their spouses all traveled to Hong Kong with their parents.

Hong Kong
October 24, 1966
Monday

Dear ones,

I hardly know where to start to tell you about the exciting 4 days in Manila. I shall start by saying that we came up to Hong Kong Sunday night about 9 P.M. The lights in the resettlement flats looked like a million Christmas trees in a forest. It was simply breathtaking. This morning early I went downtown with Sister G. to have my hair done and she left me on my own. I wandered around all by myself for 2 hours, in and out of the shops and arcades. This is the first time I have ever really seen what the shops of Hong Kong have to offer. Before, it has always just been a fast trip to Samtani's for a quick look in some exclusive shop while the driver was waiting outside. I nearly went out of my mind this morning. There are jewelry shops every five or six feet filled with pearls and jade and star sapphires for so little money and sweaters so beautifully embroidered and jeweled that it makes your head swim. And beautiful materials and snake-skin shoes and bags and suits and gorgeous blouses—linen and silk dresses all lined for $11.00. Everything is so cheap. I didn't buy a single thing, but I had a wonderful time. But all the time my heart was breaking because you were not here to see it all. I ran into two elders on their way to buy some clothes and they told me how to get back to the mission home on the bus so I took a double-decker bus back and got a wonderful look at Hong Kong all for a few pennies. This is the first time I have ever been downtown on my own and did I love it! But best of all, this is the place where we finally got mail after 3 weeks.

Now to get back to Manila. Saturday we had a meeting with the elders that took nearly all day but it was a very good one. There are now 62 elders in Manila. The new chapel is a dream. It is made of marble and dark Philippine wood and is very churchy looking. We stayed in the Manila Hotel, who were putting up President Lyndon B. Johnson and others of the leaders who came for the Summit Meeting. Saturday night Dean Rusk moved in a few doors down the hall. The place was swarming with 600 press men plus all kinds of secret service, etc. It was really exciting. By late Saturday night they had moved all the civilians out, except us, but the manager had promised President G. we could stay until Sunday morning because he is a regular customer.

President Johnson's suite was just down the hall. They weren't very anxious to let us through, but we finally talked them into it. They were completely redecorating the whole hotel. Saturday night it looked like our place the day before a home wedding: paint buckets, drop cloths, scaffolding, ladders, uncrated furniture. The President was due in Sunday afternoon, and at mid-night Saturday the place was absolute chaos. They were laying new floor in the ballroom and hanging new chandeliers, which were so huge and so beautiful they were astounding. They had laid wall-to-wall carpet in the President's bath-room, hung a crystal chandelier, and moved furniture in from the stores, which they said would all be returned after the Summit Meeting was over. At 8 o'clock Sunday morning the Assistant Secretary of State of the United States of America knocked on our hotel room door and said, "Mrs. Hinckley, I am so very sorry to rush you, but what time could we move into your room?" By this time they had put a hot line telephone in our room, with a card on it say-ing, "To reach the White House switchboard simply dial 4–2055."

Filipino boys everywhere were raking leaves, cleaning gutters, sweep-ing streets. This is probably the best thing that has ever happened to Manila. There seems to be a feeling of optimism here that something is in the wind for a settlement of the Vietnam situation. At least, there is a dead earnestness on the part of the countries coming to the Summit that something must be done to break this situation. By the time you get this letter we will know what has come of it, but there seems a determination here to bring this war to an end. They do not like it and feel that some settlement must be reached.

We dedicated the chapel in Manila Sunday morning at 10. It was origi-nally scheduled for the afternoon, but the dignitaries were scheduled to arrive every 30 minutes from 2 o'clock until 4:30. During those hours traffic was stopped at the airport and roped off on most of the boulevards and main streets. The dedication was a thrill. There were 1,000 there and they could all speak English. What a relief. I was the only woman on the program, except Sister G., who sang "Bless This House." I felt that I did better than usual. When I stood up I didn't know what in the world I was going to say, but we had the spirit with us all through the meeting and we came out just walking on air. Dad has never done better. We shook hands with the entire congregation, which was very tiring, but also very thrilling. The Filipinos are so affectionate and loving and warm. We saw many who had been at the first meeting 5 years ago. The Church is simply going wild here. There are 1800 members now and they have an average attendance of 58 percent at sacrament meeting, which is probably the highest anywhere in the world. The Church membership is increasing at the rate of 75 percent per year. The missionaries say they have the most fabulous MIA. They can throw together a program in 30 minutes that would look professional anywhere, and do they love it! They have many, many families who have been baptized, some lawyers, real estate men, a doctor, several teachers. It is just hilarious to listen to them. Their English is so funny and they are so uninhibited. Sister L. says, "I could tell da Prezidents wat to do about ze problems. Zae could all join ze Mormone Chairch."

After the dedication we went out to the G.'s again for a lovely meal and then they took us to the airport in their two Cadillacs, the black one and the white one. We got there just too late to see President Johnson arrive, but his plane was still on the platform. We did see the president of Australia arrive in the big beautiful Qantas plane. It was quite thrilling. They had a very colorful marching unit in blue and white and gold, and long red carpet strips out on the runway. We got a good look at President Marcos and his elegant wife in her pale yellow formal with the big butterfly sleeves as they greeted the visitors. The whole thing was very colorful and exciting. By the time we got to Hong Kong I felt as if I had lived nine days in one.

Thank you, thank you, thank you for your letters. After three weeks I was getting to the point where I was dreaming about all of you every night. They were terrible nightmarish dreams, so it was wonderful to hear from each of you and be reassured that all is well. I just wish I could enjoy this without wishing so much that you were here. It is so terrible to have all this fun alone. I think I have loved it more this time than ever before. I know I have never enjoyed Manila so much, and Hong Kong never seemed so wonderful as it did this morning. Let's all plan to come together sometime. I love every street in this crazy city. We are all going out to dinner tonight. The mission presidents' seminar starts tomorrow and continues for 3 days. I think then that Sister H. and I will stay here while the men go to Vietnam. I hope so. I just can't get enough of this place. I wish I had a million dollars to spend, but it is fun just to look at everything.

Be good children and work hard, so you can earn a lot of money and see this gorgeous, wonderful world and meet all these wonderful people. It is the greatest thing in the world to be a Latter-day Saint. I am sure you know what I mean. Dad and I miss you all very much and we are proud of each one of you.

M

octubre*October 23, 1967*

Dear Everyone,

I am typing 5 carbon copies on an electric typewriter. It's a challenge.

We are in Hong Kong today. Beautiful weather. Dashed down to Samtani's right after breakfast. He opened up at 8:30 especially for Dad. He picked out two beautiful pieces of material and when we went back at 3 p.m. for a fitting, we found that he had mistakenly cut them to Clark's measurements. Too bad Clark isn't where they could be sent to him. The whole process starts over now with another fitting at 7 p.m.

We met with the missionaries this morning at 9:30. There are only 38 left, 10 of whom are local Chinese. In a way, this is a blessing in disguise, as Dad has long thought that the number in Hong Kong was much too high. The mission president himself now says that this 38 is an ideal number for Hong Kong. The calling of the local Chinese to fulfill missions will greatly strengthen the branches when they are released.

We had one of those marvelous meetings this morning. Every missionary here is humble and sweet and loving the work and thoroughly dedicated. They are doing the work that was formerly done by 90 missionaries, so they are extremely busy, which adds to their happiness. Being few in numbers has also brought about a very close feeling of unity.

We had a meeting with the Chinese Saints yesterday afternoon at Gum Tong hall over on the island. It was a good meeting and lots of fun to visit with everyone.

Things have quieted down in Hong Kong, although a bomb went off last night in front of the branch hall during a farewell testimonial for one of the local missionaries. I wasn't there, but the elders said it was quite a thrill. We have discovered, however, that it isn't quite as dangerous as it sounds, because they plant the bombs in plain sight with signs that read, "This is a bomb." The police are called and they set it off. Some police have been injured, but that's about all recently.

Samtani has invited everyone (all 54 of us) to dinner on the house tomorrow night. When he made the offer Dad snatched him up on it before he told him there would be 54, but he didn't bat an eyelash. Said he would take any number up to 100. Tourist business is down considerably in Hong Kong and the bargaining is supposed to be pretty good. Dad said he would go shopping with me tomorrow so that ought to be good for a little fun. It is really much better now for shopping because the streets and shops are noticeably quieter. All I need is money. I would like to get linen for all of you, but it is a worry to get it home, as they have been confiscating anything that even looks like it could be from China, so I will forego that.

Everyone around this mission home got mail today, except me. Unless something shows up by Wednesday when we leave here I am afraid some-one will be getting an $8.00 phone call collect. Dick is the only one of you from whom we have heard.

Dad did a superb job with the elders this morning. He talked from the scriptures more than usual, but it was beautifully done and it was one of his better days.

So far, the trip has been quite leisurely, especially for me—not so much so for Dad, of course, but we have stayed about 3 days in each place with a good night's rest each night. This has been a blessing, but from here on I hate to think of what it will be.

Love to all of you,

M

August 6, 1971

Dear Fam,

The biggest challenge so far is getting a letter written. Stayed with G.'s at temple during youth conference from Saturday to Thursday. Got our speech making over with at the Sunday session so the remainder was quite enjoyable. Monday and Tuesday the 970 youth practiced for the road show and dance festivals, which were held at night, so Jane and I walked the streets of Berne during these 2 days and looked in the shops. Wednesday everyone went on a chartered train into the Swiss Alps where they disembarked for various hikes. Most of them hiked to the town of Grindelwald and some over the hill to Interlaken, but a few of us "older ones" took an additional train ride up the mountain. When we arrived we climbed a few feet up the glacier and stood in the midst of the most enormous expanse of snow you could imagine. It was fantastic! Also went inside of the mountain to the ice palace. Had a delicious meal at a restaurant up on the mountain and then took the train back to Interlaken, where everyone met and boarded the chartered train back to Berne.

Forgot to say that Monday the G.'s drove us up into the green, green mountains covered with Swiss chalets. Then took a gondola straight up to a little tiny Swiss village where we walked around and looked at the vegetable gardens and flowers and had lunch at an outdoor restaurant surrounded with the world's most beautiful scenery. This was the first look at the Swiss mountain scenery for Dad and he enjoyed it immensely.

Thursday morning Jane slept in while Dad and I went to a temple session, and then Jane and I took the fast train back into Berne for one last look. On the way home we got off the train too soon and had a long hike into Zollikofen. It was sad to leave Berne. We loved it.

Left the G.'s Thursday afternoon and drove with President and Sister P. to Freiberg, in So. Germany, where the mission tour starts. When we arrived Thursday night we walked for an hour or so through the town square and around the cathedral. It was very quaint and beautiful. Today (Friday) we have been all day at the chapel with the missionaries. Jane gave her first talk and did very well, but shook like a leaf when it was over.

Weather, for the most part, has been delightful.

We will be leaving the chapel here in Freiberg as soon as Dad finishes the interviews and should arrive in Munich after dark—6 hours on the autobahn.

We are having a marvelous time. Jane is loving it. The Swiss mission president had 4 grown children at the youth conference. The president from Frankfurt had a seventeen-year-old daughter. That made it much better for Jane, as she could not communicate in German. The funniest was watching her dance with a German boy in dead silence. The language barrier is horrible.

Saturday afternoon

Today we are in Stuttgart, home of Mercedes-Benz. Stuttgart is a European edition of San Francisco, without the water. It is a city built on hills, quite picturesque.

Mission tour ended yesterday (Friday) with an all-day meeting, starting at 9 o'clock and ending at 6 P.M. Great relief. It has been a hard week, going through the same routine every day in a different city. For a while in the afternoons while Dad was interviewing and the missionaries were conducting workshops, Jane and Sister P. and I would walk the streets and nap in the car. We did have Wednesday off, but wouldn't you know Dad got sick so we didn't go to any of the fancy castles. During the afternoon when he got feeling a little better we rode out to Dachau, the German prison camp where thousands of Jews were exterminated. The huge ovens and barracks still stand. It was grim.

We are holed up in a little hotel in Stuttgart today, as we have to stay for the district conference with the servicemen tomorrow (Sunday). Jane and I walked the streets for about 4 hours, then promptly at 2 p.m. this huge city folded up. Supermarkets, bookstores, bicycle shops, fruit stands—everything was folded down within 10 minutes and a great exodus of people moved toward the train station. It was something to see. We dragged ourselves back up the streets and steps through the heat to our hotel. The missionaries were waiting so I went back to the chapel with them and sat in on some leadership meetings for Relief Society, Primary, and MIA for servicemen's branches. The district president of Primary has no counselors, secretary, or anything.

She is a one-man show. There is not one branch Primary presidency fully organized. Just not enough people to go around.

Next week should be very exciting. We leave early Monday (6 a.m.) for Salzburg and Vienna, then on to Milan and Florence. We will ride the train all day Tuesday from Vienna to Milan. Dad expects to use this day to prepare his Manchester conference talk.

Prices in Germany are outrageous. I paid $4.50 for a hairdo. The American dollar has devaluated here seriously. Many beautiful clothes in the shop windows, but outrageous prices.

We are missing the children like crazy. Jane is already scheming how she can get back to Switzerland next year. Apparently there are plenty of jobs for waitresses in that summer vacation land.

Love,

M

Dear Kathy,

I had forgotten what a long ride it is to Hong Kong: 8½ hours from Tokyo to Hong Kong. So grateful for the layover in Honolulu and a night's rest in Tokyo. J. and A. met us in Tokyo and took us to a hotel in town where we visited for a couple of hours, until our heads were swimming with sleepiness. Dad and A. pored over maps and talked of stake divisions. J. and I talked of the perils of raising children when the parents are in Tokyo and the children in Hawaii.

Next morning we had a good flight down to Hong Kong. Finished the "Dead Sea Scrolls" just before Hong Kong came into view. Beautiful day, 65 degree temperatures and sunshine. The harbor was alive with boats—large and small. The daily laundry flying from all the balconies—noise and millions of people. It never changes, but it is much more delightful in January than in the steamy rains of August.

Went directly to the mission home where we had 15 minutes to prepare to leave for a meeting with the missionaries over on the island. Met in the beautiful old English home "Gumtong Hall" (the McCune Mansion of Hong Kong). Back to the mission home and dinner and family home evening with the W.'s. The stake president of Hong Kong came over and talked with Dad about the stake. He looks much more relaxed and happy than on the day he was sustained.

Wednesday morning we were scheduled to go over to Macau in the hydra-foil to see the 4 missionaries who could not come to the meeting on Tuesday, but Dad begged off. The mission presidents were beginning to arrive and he wanted to begin his interviews with them. This gave us a couple of hours in the morning to go to Nathan Road and mingle with the masses. I got a new Seiko watch. So good to know the time of day again, and helpful when traveling with such a "punctual" companion. Dad then went over to the hotel on the Ferry and I stayed to shop alone at the Oceans Terminal. Bought the Pearce girls a Chinese costume per Ginny's instruction.

Wednesday we were all day in the seminar at Lee Gardens Hotel on the island. Sat too long and ate too much. Wednesday night Dad went to a priesthood meeting to ordain a patriarch in the Hong Kong Stake. Mission presidents all went out to an area to see the Chinese visitors center. I had seen it so I stayed in the hotel room to do laundry.

Thursday morning we had a "Sister session" for 2 hours and then reconvened with the brethren. I slipped out for a shampoo during the translation department discussion. Happiness is clean hair.

Love,

M

Dear Family,

It is Sunday afternoon in Coimbature, India. We have 3 hours to rest before another meeting tonight. My body is so tired I can hardly move it an inch but my eyes are wide open. We are having a rare experience again . . . not unlike the one we had here 12 years ago.

Friday morning we left Hong Kong and flew to Bangkok. The next morning we had breakfast with mission assistants and a couple of young Thai leaders who had been to BYU–Hawaii. From there to the fine chapel erected mostly by American servicemen, where we had a 2-hour meeting with 100 missionaries. There was only one Thai missionary among them. They are greatly missing the strength of the U.S. military members since they were all evacuated. One wonders if the whole organization would collapse if the missionaries had to leave. Among the missionaries was a fine young man, a clown from Barnum and Bailey Circus. He keeps the missionaries in stitches with his pantomimes.

At noon we climbed aboard Malaysian Airlines and flew for 3 hours to Kuala Lumpur, the capital of Malaysia. This is a place we had not been before. We were met by the president of the Singapore Mission and a family from Idaho who are there with the Bureau of Reclamation with 4 children, all of whom are attending the International School and loving it. These young people do a great job of living happily in a strange world without becoming a part of it.

The P.'s drove us around Kuala Lumpur for an hour. There are beautiful parks, buildings, and heavy tropical foliage. We had dinner at the P. home which is a huge castle-like house with fountains, marble floors, and circular stairways. After dinner 49 members gathered at the home for a meeting. They set up a pulpit and folding chairs in the grand entrance hall and there was room to spare. This was the first visit of a General Authority to Malaysia. Present were Malaysians, East Indians, Chinese, Canadians, and Americans. We met a beautiful blonde woman whose father is a bishop in Australia and whose husband is a rich Chinese non-member. She teaches her children the entire Church program by herself as they live up-country where there are no other members. There were two Malaysian girls who have been active for 3 years—one is a counselor in Relief Society, and the other is the Cultural Refinement teacher. Neither is baptized because they cannot get parental permission. One is planning to be married July 24, 1979, in the Salt Lake Temple. Her fiancé is a member. Hope she makes it.

Next morning we left early for India. We stopped on the way to the airport to walk among the rubber trees where they were harvesting the sap that is made into rubber. Also saw large palm-oil plantations. At the airport we looked at Malaysian handicrafts and I bought a spoon which I will send. Many tin mines are here from which they make beautiful pewter ware. The saints gave us a small pewter plate with an inscription on it.

Our flight to India was in a small crowded plane and uncomfortable. Dad read "Upstairs in the White House" all the way. I read the Old Testament. It is my 1977 project and is surprisingly interesting reading.

The plane came down in Madras and a Mormon couple were there to visit with us. They have been on four overseas assignments since graduating from BYU in "foreign affairs." They now have four little boys and have never lived in the States. She just had a huge box of supplies arrive from Church distribution with all the Sunday School manuals and Primary supplies and was very excited.

We are staying in a place which was a private club for the English in the days of English occupation. It looks like the Foreign Legion slept here in 1800 and nothing has changed. Same plumbing, same mosquito netting over the four-poster beds. The towels have turned grey with age. The pattern has worn off the china dishes and the barefoot turbaned Indians run in and out of the room filling water glasses and turning fans off and on and shining our shoes.

P. T., who started the work here years ago, is still working his head off. He has baptized over 200 people but they are such childlike people that the work never gets off the ground. In 12 years they have learned 2 hymns, "Abide With Me" and "God Be With You Till We Meet Again," which they sing at the opening of the meetings. We went to a meeting out in a village Saturday night and we could see some little progress from 12 years ago. At least the chanting and drum beating was replaced with the 2 hymns and they were meeting in a small hut built for the purpose instead of under the trees. The hut had been swept clean as a pin and was decorated with many colors of twisted crepe paper streamers. A picture of Jesus and a picture of the First Presidency hung on the walls. We sat on a bench covered with an old "white" dishtowel. The members (about 30) sat on the floor.

P. took us to his home where he seated us in his living room (about 6' x 10'), placed two stools in front of us, covered them with an old towel, and proceeded to serve us the goodies his wife had spent all day making. Dad tried to beg off but I gave him a big nudge and he agreed to have just "a very little" of each item.

We went from there to the orphanage where P. takes in unwanted children until he can arrange for their adoption. He is placing them in homes in the U.S. (mostly Utah) and in Sweden. It was a sobering experience. The tiny new babies were lying in a row on mats placed on the concrete floor. They were so skinny and weak they looked more dead than alive. I thought of our beautiful lively happy little David and Jonathan and Annie and it made me sick inside.

This morning (Sunday) we held meetings in 3 more villages. Two of them had little buildings—the third had put up a bowery. These groups were not using the hymns, but were singing some strange sort of Indian music. The group leader had to be told every word to say as he conducted the meetings. Dad is going to have a long talk with P. this evening and we will then go out to one more village for the last meeting.

Life here is not like going back 100 years but like going back to Old Testament days. Women are all dressed in saris. White horned cows and donkeys carrying their burdens, women filling their jugs at the well and carrying them back to their huts . . .

The street sights are beyond description. I think of my elaborate home in America and wonder what the Lord thinks of our living in such opulence. On the other hand, the Lord has provided the good things of the earth for the benefit of his people—if only the good things could be more evenly distributed.

Later—Sunday afternoon

We just went over to meet about 12 people who came about 80 miles from the north to see us. One is a baptized member. The others are requesting baptism. They all are a very bright educated family. Dad interviewed them for baptism and recommended them highly to the mission president. This is a very different group from the villagers and the most encouraging experience of the past two days.

P. T. has a 17-year-old daughter who is hoping to go to BYU–Hawaii next Fall. She is taking some entrance test next week. She speaks very little English, is so shy but a sweet little thing with a long black braid and pretty white teeth. I can't imagine how she will bridge the culture gap. She looks beautiful in her saris and gold jewelry. I can't imagine her in Western clothes. She is so frightened. Four years in Hawaii is a long time and thousands of miles from home. In the next world I hope something can be done about the separation of families. Maybe that's what the gospel is all about.

Tomorrow morning we head out for Cairo, and it will be a long ride with a 3-hour layover in Bangalore. We will be in Cairo for 2½ days, and since there will be only one group of members to hold a meeting with we are hoping to see a few sights if our tired bodies can still walk.

Love,

M

Dear Family,

It was a long and tedious ride from India to Cairo—about 22 hours with stops at Bangalore, Bombay, and Pakistan. In Bangalore we had 3 hours so we walked out of the airport and through the streets for an hour. Bangalore is in the interior where tourists are novelties, and we were followed by staring children. Not a white face did we see nor a western dress. Even the women working on road construction were wearing saris. In Bombay we walked from the airport to a fine hotel not far away and had a leisurely supper. In Pakistan we only had 40 minutes and spent it looking at the fantastic things in the airport gift shop. Finally at 3 a.m. we arrived in Cairo. Actually it was 7 a.m. by our watches. We had flown all day and all night and we were glassy-eyed. We went first to the customs counter. We could see our friends the H.'s waiting for us through the glass doors but it was more than an hour later that we got through to them.

We later learned that the H.'s were under surveillance by the secret police for proselyting among Muslims, which is strictly against the law. (Actually they were innocent, but were under suspicion.) To make a long story short, a letter Dad had written to the H.'s concerning our arrival had apparently been intercepted, and the Bureau of Investigation took over as soon as we arrived at the customs counter. They removed all of Dad's papers, including his little black notebook, and began to pore over them. Even the laundry marks on his shirts were scrutinized. He had dictated his daily diary on tapes and they took all of those. The entire plane load of people stood in line during all of this for the better part of an hour while we were interrogated. Finally, they figured there was no way they could read through all of his papers so they said they would have to keep them for a couple of days. We did not get them back until we left Cairo on Thursday and we felt lucky to get them back at all. They returned all but one tape.

There are 3 Mormons from the States teaching at the American University in Cairo and they were warned and threatened with their dismissal from the country if they did not cease and desist their religious activities. The police had been paying the H.'s a few friendly calls so we held the first meeting with the American members at one of the professor's homes and the next night at H.'s for investigators. The professors did not want to chance that at their home, but the H.'s are fearless. Needless to say, it was an experience. I might add that the H.'s are only proselyting among the Christians, which is not against the law, so they do not worry too much, but Dad was plenty nervous about the whole thing because if the police want to get sticky they could refuse to renew the H.'s visa and they could be in real trouble, as he has made a huge investment in a business there.

But enough of that—we had a very interesting time in Cairo. The pyramids are truly one of the wonders of the world and it was a fantastic experience to climb up inside. We visited ruins and museums and marketplaces and monasteries and saw unbelievable sights. Our hotel overlooked the beautiful Nile River. It is a dirty mad city but oh so interesting. Camels, donkeys, and goats and taxi cabs and millions of Arabs. The H.'s are doing some research on where the Holy Family was purported to have been when they took the Baby Jesus to Egypt. He showed us a street where tradition says they traveled down to the Nile and crossed over. If they can get enough information they will do an article for the *Ensign* on it. I had just read the story of Joseph in Egypt and the exodus led by Moses, so I was double thrilled with all we saw. We watched them make papyri paper and saw a lot of treasures from King Tut's tomb, but the climb inside the pyramids was the greatest. They have a "Sound and Light" production at the base of the pyramids and sphinx every night, similar to what they do in Athens, but we were holding meetings both nights so didn't see it.

Got into London at midnight last night and British Air put us up at a hotel in town. We got up early and walked down Oxford Street and oh, it did feel so wonderful to be back in London, where everyone speaks English and the names of streets and stores are familiar and where the shop windows are so breathtakingly beautiful. After the dirt of India and Egypt it was like being in heaven. It was raining a little, but not very cold. We bought Dad a hat in Selfridges and then went over to Marks and Spencers to get his year's supply of shirts. Took a taxi over to Hyde Park Chapel to see the B.'s. They drove us over to see the new quarters for BYU semester abroad. England is green again. Another 2 hours and we will be in Chicago where the weather is 7 below zero with a wind. It has been a fantastic trip. We have not been sick a day. We should get home tonight if we make our connection. Dad has to go to Phoenix, Arizona, in the morning to stake conference.

Hope all is well.

Love,

M

Dear Barneses,

The past four days are a blur. Can't remember what we did when, but it has all been exciting. I thought 5 days to roam London would be what I have been waiting for all these years, but find it is hardly enough time to turn around, and many of the things I planned to do will have to be postponed until the next time around.

Wednesday morning Sister F. took Dad and me to the opening of the Chelsea flower show—supposed to be the best and most prestigious flower show in the world. The lineup was two blocks long, but what we could see over the heads and through the shoulders of the mobs of people was spectacular. Five hundred to 1,000 roses in many of the bouquets. Delphinium 8 feet tall. The displays were dramatic. We must have stayed 2 hours and only saw a small part.

In the afternoon we headed for Marks and Spencers to replenish his supply of white shirts. Dad's never happier than when he is riding the London underground without a chaperone.

9 days later—at home

After life for a week with the F.'s this home routine is pretty grim. She has a live-in "kitchen girl," a Filipino woman who takes charge of the kitchen, cooking all the meals and serving them and keeping the kitchen in a state of gleaming sterility. The cleaning lady comes twice a week, the driver keeps the cars shined and does some of the errand running. All Sister F. does is the shopping (every morning at the market at 7 a.m. when the fruit and vegetables shipped from Israel and Italy are at their best), makes out the menus, reports to the kitchen help how many there will be for dinner, and she is then free for the day.

Saturday morning Sister F. took us (the women) to the grocery store where the queen shops, Fortnum & Masons. It is near Piccadilly and you must surely include it on your next tour of London. Red carpet, crystal chandeliers, and clerks dressed in full formal attire, striped pants and tail coats. Many fancy people were shopping there, and there are many items other than food.

Saturday afternoon Dad and I rode down to Romford for the stake conference with the regional representative and his wife. I have met them several times, but never have spent any time with his wife. While the men were busy she drove me around Romford in the busy Saturday afternoon traffic. We passed an open-air market, so we parked the car along with all the produce trucks surrounding the place and wandered through the stalls for more than an hour. There were crowds of people as if there would never be any merchandise available from that day on. Sister H. is the typical, lovely, English lady who went to a finishing school and refers to Walt

Disney as Walter Disney. Saturday night we went to the stake conference and then drove back to London, arriving about 11 p.m.

Sunday morning was a beautiful sunny day in London. Six stakes from the London area met in the Royal Albert Concert Hall where boundaries were rearranged and the six stakes were made into nine stakes. It was a beautiful sight to see more than 4,000 members gathered in Royal Albert Hall. It is a magnificent old building with five tiers of balconies, red velvet drapes, and gold filigree. Dad went to hear Fritz Kreisler play the violin there 45 years ago and sat up in the 5th balcony. Little did he dream that someday he would be sitting on the stand conducting a meeting with 4,000 members. He was excited and emotional. This was one of those occasions that we will always remember.

Monday we flew to Detroit, went on a picnic with Clark and Kathleen and the children. It was lovely and I am glad we took the time. We were home by noon on Tuesday and Dad had meetings that afternoon. It took me about four days to get over the terrible, tired, lazy feeling.

Dad had to begin immediately to prepare a talk for the dedication of the new Visitors' Center on Temple Square on Thursday. It is beautiful, and impressive. Thank goodness he did not have an appointment this weekend. We worked our ankle bones off in the yard on Saturday. The weeds were taking over and the roses infected with bugs. Sometimes condominium living has great appeal.

Love,

Mom

Dear ones,

So far, so good. We are all well and happy and are having a great time. The Young Ambassadors are a wonderful group of young people to be with and they make friends with the Chinese wherever we go. Their program is loud, colorful, jazzy, fast-moving and Dad has sat through every performance without complaint.

The concerts are a complete sell-out with people jamming the doors trying to get in. At the end the audiences simply go wild, swarming up on the stage trying to get near the performers.

Peking was not what I expected. I suppose I thought it would be like Hong Kong or San Francisco Chinatown. It is a far cry from either. A bleak place. Everything painted asphalt grey—not a blade of grass or flower or green shrub to be seen. No cars. Millions of bicycles and shabby old busses packed with Chinese all wearing the same uniform: dark slacks and dark jackets. No wonder they go crazy over the show—beautiful costumes, beautiful girls, beautiful music.

We arrived in Nanking at 4 a.m. this morning after a 15-hour train ride from Peking. A very different place—beautiful green and roses everywhere. There was a performance this afternoon at the teachers college for 1,000 or more students. As usual they got a tremendous response. The entertainers memorized many of the songs in Chinese and also memorized all the introductions of the numbers in Chinese. The audiences love it! We could scarcely get on the busses after the performance today for the crowds who wanted to talk. If only missionaries could get in here they would never have to knock on doors. These people are so curious. Wherever we go, a crowd gathers within minutes. After the show this afternoon one group of students asked if it was because of Jesus Christ that these young people were so lively and happy.

This is a very different trip for us. Dad has no responsibilities and goes around in grey slacks, blue shirt, and blue blazer. I scarcely know him. Most impressive was the Great Wall of China, one of the wonders of the world. It goes for 3,000 miles through the mountains. We hiked up the wall (it is wide enough for 6-span horses) to a lookout point which takes about 3 hours and was a monumental effort, one flight of steps after another. Some of our party did not make it all the way, but we had our pride to deal with. It was a warm spring day and about 10,000 Chinese had the same idea.

We will leave the group a week from today and go back to Hong Kong to divide the stake and then to Korea for a reorganization. Dad got a message Saturday asking him to go to Sapporo, Japan, for a reorganization also. This will delay us for a couple of days, getting us home about June 5th.

Tomorrow we take a 4-hour train ride to Shanghai. I can scarcely believe it.

Weather is magnificent.

Love,

Mom

Letters to Grandchildren

*M*arjorie Hinckley's love for her family extended to all the genera-tions, and with letters and cards she helped maintain family ties as her rapidly growing posterity spread across the globe. The few sample letters in this section, selected from the many she sent to her twenty-five grandchildren, show her love and interest in them. Lines from Christmas cards, though brief, set the tone for the season and helped the children feel its magic. Finally, postcards from her many travels demonstrate her keen ability to hone in on little details that would be of interest to a child. She knew what it would mean to her grandchildren to know that she was always thinking of them, no matter what else she was doing in the world. What greater testimony could they have of their importance to her?

The Hinckleys at home with many of their grandchildren

Celia was nearly ten years old when this letter was written.

September 9, 1976
Thursday

Dear Celia,

I just hung up the phone from talking with your mother when your letter arrived this afternoon. Glad to hear you have an individual class this year. It is probably much better than the team teaching you had last year. I can scarcely imagine Jeff trotting off to school with you in the mornings. Does he have recess at the same time as you? Probably not.

Ginny and Jim are going on a 2-day anniversary getaway to Snowbird Friday and Saturday. I will take care of Amy and Heidi. The others are going to Janie's. Wish you were here. Amy can take several steps now, but drops to her knees when she wants to get someplace fast.

Jonathan was named last Sunday. Everyone was there, including all the Dudleys. I had not been in the new chapel on the bend and thought it was lovely—cozy and churchie. After the meeting Jane served a lovely dinner to 26 people on the front yard. She handled it like a pro. We were all impressed.

Grandpa is going to Canada early Saturday morning, but I will not be lonely with Amy and Heidi and peaches and pears to put up.

Love

M

Marjorie writes in this letter to ten-year-old Jeff a story about his cousins' grandparents that would be appealing to a boy of that age. Katie is his younger sister.

January 18, 1980

Dear Jeff,

I finally got the bookmark which you made and was delighted. It is very clever indeed and will be a real conversation piece. I am using it in my scriptures as I carry these with me a great deal and this gives me a chance to show it off.

Since you and Jonathan left, poor Michael is surrounded by girls at all family get-togethers. It will be better when James learns to walk and talk.

Mr. Pearce was robbed last night out at his yard. Two men with ski masks and gloves climbed over the high fence and broke the door in. They squirted tear gas in Grandpa Pearce's face and threw him on the bed while they went through everything. They apparently didn't find anything they wanted except his wallet with over $300.00 in it. Grandma Pearce is very distraught over the whole thing, but Grandpa Pearce is just plain *mad!*

It was wonderful to have Katie for a day and get acquainted with her. She was with me all day until 5 p.m. before she spoke a word, but once she started she talked a blue streak until Grandpa came home and then she went into silence again. What a funny little person.

Kathleen has been here with Ada Christine for 4 days. Christine is the carbon copy of Holly. We put them on the plane at 7:00 this morning.

Have a fun day!

Love,

Grandma H.

Celia was serving a mission in Bueno Aires, Argentina, at this time.

Sao Paulo, Brazil
April 24, 1988

Dear Celia,

How we would love to play hooky and skip down to Argentina. We are so close and yet so far.

Saturday morning we arrived in Rio feeling like walking zombies. You know all about it. The men showered and went to the 4-hour meeting with the priesthood members. The women attempted to do a little sight-seeing, but visibility was poor because of fog and we ended up walking through a shopping mall, just like home only thousands and thousands of people.

We had a wonderful area conference this morning in a large sports center with 4,000 people and a tremendous choir of 350. Best of all was a meeting with some 200 missionaries at 8:00 a.m. before the conference. On the front row sat 12 sister missionaries. It choked me up. I could just see you in that setting and I felt so happy and proud. One sister from California cried during the entire meeting. I tried to get to her after but lost her in the crowd.

After the conference we boarded an ancient prop-jet and flew for one hour to Sao Paulo, a little metropolis of 15 million people (the third largest city in the world). The men have gone to a special meeting with some priesthood brethren. I am spending the evening in the elaborate condo occupied by the area presidency. We think the Church Administration Building is a pretty impressive high-rise, but there are 16 such buildings in this walled compound where we are staying.

The young man who translated for Grandpa this morning was the first black man to go on a mission after the revelation which gave them the priesthood. He was engaged to be married and had mailed invitations for the wedding, and when the revelation was given his fiancée said, "This is what you have always wanted. Now you can go on a mission. I will wait for you." They postponed their wedding for 2 years. There are some tremendous people in Brazil. Many of them stood for 2 hours during the conference this morning.

When we were planning this trip I could hardly get myself geared up for it. Now that I am here, I think what I would have missed if I had not come. We will be visiting other cities in Brazil during the week, meeting with members and investigators and missionaries. I love these missionaries so much I can hardly keep from crying when I see them. They are absolutely tremendous.

Your third letter came the day we left and your mother read it to me on the phone. We were so happy to hear from you. Every night when Grandpa walks in the house his first words are, "Did they get any mail from Celia today?" Every night when he prays he says, "Please, please, bless the missionaries and especially Celia." Know that you are loved. We are so thankful you have a good first companion. That will prepare you for anything you will have to face in the future.

Affectionately,

Grandma H.

Another letter to the Hinckleys' missionary granddaughter kept Celia informed about the family, especially her siblings Jeff and Angela.

January 8, 1989

Dear Celia,

Here we are eight days into the new year. Another Christmas has come and gone. For you it was a Christmas different from any other. For us it was even different, as we were so caught up in moving, we never really got it together. We did manage to have the dinner and fish pond, and a sleepover for the younger ones, but other than that all else was postponed until next year. We had many speaking appointments during December, two of them on Christmas Day. The weather was such that we never would have made it to the places where we were supposed to be except for our trusty four-wheel drive Wagoneer, whose age is showing. We never did get out to see our families because of the weather, so it was not the usual celebration, but still a time of rejoicing and counting our blessings. Thank you for the very darling adorable Christmas card you sent with the sweet message.

As I look back on our encounter in San Rafael it somehow seems unreal—like something I dreamed. Of all the blessings of 1988, and there were many, that was the greatest. Someday I hope you have a beautiful granddaughter or handsome grandson go on a mission. Only then will you know what joy it is to see the next generation carrying the torch. We were so proud to see how much you are loved and respected by the entire mission, including the members. It is one thing to go on a mission, but another thing to magnify the calling as you have done and are doing. Our joy in you knows no bounds. Having seen you in action in Argentina we now know that there is nothing in this world that you cannot accomplish. How blessed we are that you belong to us.

During 1988 we made 5 trips overseas, plus many others in the States. This year we only have one assignment overseas, but many in the States. This means less travel, less jet lag, and more time home, which will be a welcome relief. We go to New Zealand and Australia in November, but at this point that seems a long way down the road, so we are going to enjoy the next few months.

Grandpa went to New Mexico this weekend to a regional conference and I stayed home. It is the first opportunity I have had to come up for air since returning from Argentina, and was much appreciated. However, he stopped in Arizona to see our little family there, so I did miss out on that.

Jeff seems to like his after-school job of delivering prescriptions for the drug store. He is getting to know all the streets and byways in the valley and all the old ladies with ailments. However, he sprained his ankle on the basketball floor last night, so he will be on crutches for a couple of days.

We are very proud of Angela and the super job she is doing for Murdock Travel. She is working very hard, but having considerable success in getting some good accounts for them. She is very sharp, just like her missionary sister.

We are all anxiously awaiting the stork's arrival in St. Louis. Your mother is all set to take off for the big event.

The Tabernacle Choir is singing at the inauguration in Washington, D.C., and if the weather is tolerable Jane will go back and take Jessica and Sarah on January 19th. You have heard, of course, that the United States is getting a new president by the name of Bush. Don't want you to get too far out of date.

Much love,

Grandma H.

P.S. We *love* our new apartment. Grandpa gets home for lunch frequently.

Marjorie took care to keep her granddaughter Celia up to date on the cousins closest to her age.

February 22, 1989

Dear Hermana Celia,

Your letters are wonderful. I am so grateful your mother shares them with me. Hope you don't mind.

Following is a quote from Brigham Young to a missionary son in England:

"I wish you to live and fare as the poor elders do. Grub your way along as they do and thoroughly learn how poor folks live, for you are young and hearty and can endure it and it will prove of great future benefit to you. I glory in your grit."

I glory in your grit, but we do not want you to be sick while there, nor after you return. Use wisdom.

Two weeks ago we had the privilege of speaking at a devotional for the Salt Lake Temple workers. Over 1,000 of them. It was a moving experience to see the beautiful upstairs assembly room in the temple filled with people dressed in white. Last Sunday we had the same experience in the Hawaii Temple, except it was held in the celestial room, since there is no assembly room in that temple. The meeting was relayed by screen to all the other rooms in the temple.

We had 3 full days in Laie for BYU meetings, devotionals, firesides, missionary zone conferences, etc., etc. It is not acceptable for parents to brag about their children, but perfectly acceptable for grandparents to brag about their grandchildren, so I told the missionaries about my beautiful granddaughter in Argentina and about some of the successes you have had. I did not mention the hard times as they are completely overlooked and overshadowed by the good times. Right?

Had a nice visit on the phone with Rosemary. I am convinced she has a good marriage and is happy. She is in the right circumstance for her at this time, and you are in the right circumstance for you at this time.

Laura is in California for 10 days with the dance group. She works her head off to keep up with her studies, but is doing remarkably well. With Laura at BYU and Rosemary married and David in Sweden, Emily is very sad and lonely. Laura is thinking of coming home for the summer and taking some classes at BYU Salt Lake extension. This will be so good for Emily, as she is also considering summer school.

As soon as we arrived home from Hawaii, Grandpa began work on a satellite talk for next Sunday. He shuts himself in his study every night and I have to pretend he is not home. There is no letup ever, but what a blessing to be involved in the greatest work on the face of the earth. We have a wonderful life.

Love you!

Grandma

Jennie had gone to England to live with a mission president's family and help with their children.

May 13, 1989

Dear Jennie,

We absolutely loved your letter. I read it three times to be sure I hadn't missed anything. Sounds like you are coping well and all your concerns about the cooking etc. have been overcome, although a little challenge every day is a good thing. Your descriptions of England are so vivid I can see and smell the place—the rain, the green, and the picture postcard scenes everywhere one looks. How I love that place! Maybe I love it because *all,* and I mean *all,* of my ancestors came from there and it gives me a sense of "home." They came from all over the place—Liverpool, London, Cambridge, Brighton, the Cliffs of Dover.

I am enclosing a more detailed life of Sarah Jarrold than you have perhaps read or heard. Since she came from Cambridge, I thought it might hold a little interest for you at this particular time. She was the first on my matriarchal line to join the Church.

I might mention that *"Reader's Digest"* last month had a wonderful article on Margaret Thatcher. If you did not see it let me know and I will send it to you as you certainly should read it now that you are an Englishman.

We are in Lovell, Wyoming, this weekend for an area conference. This is Buffalo Bill territory. The people are wonderful! It is so good for Grandpa to get out with the people where there is faith and commitment and testimony.

The twins had their 20th birthday in April, and right on the heels of that, Rosemary turned 22, so we have been to some great birthday dinners at the Pearces.

Your mother went all out for your dad's birthday and had a delicious dinner on the deck. Jodi was a doll the way she was buzzing around serving everyone and clearing away dishes.

Rosemary is taking 20 hours this quarter and working part-time on campus. She is pushing hard endeavoring to finish this August, but is wondering what she is going to do with her hard-earned political science major once she gets it.

Heidi has decided to go to Ricks. She has an excellent scholarship there and seems to want a smaller school.

Grandpa's prayers have been modified slightly. He used to say "Bless all of our loved ones, particularly Celia in Argentina." Now he says "Bless our loved ones, particularly Celia in Argentina and Jennie in England." We love you and miss you more than you can imagine, but are thrilled that you are where you are, doing what you are doing.

May 18, 1989

One more addition to this packet—your Mother's Day letter written on the 10th and mailed on the 12th arrived in today's mail. One week, which is quite wonderful service all the way from Coventry.

This was a letter to warm my heart. This was a letter to make any rough roads we might have traveled to reach age 77 worth it all. You gave me a Mother's Day supreme. A wonderful letter and a phone call.

I ask myself what I ever could have done to deserve such a remarkable and beautiful and wonderful granddaughter. I sometimes think you are too good to be true. When I hear the sad stories from some of my friends of their grandchildren and the anxious days and nights of parents and grandparents I look at you and marvel. If only everyone in the world could have a granddaughter like you, what joy there would be in the world.

I don't know what to say except "I love you," and that seems so inadequate. Thank you for being what you are and for bringing so much joy into our lives.

Grandma

Since writing this letter in the hotel room in Lovell, Wyoming, last weekend, we have talked to you on the phone. My heart leaped when I heard your voice. I could scarcely believe it! And then to have your family here was a stroke of luck. What a Mother's Day for all of us! The connection was so clear it was as if you were right here. It was reassuring to realize that you are as near as the telephone.

Apparently you have not seen too much of England yet, but as time goes on you will see more and more of it. Just to be there and "feel" it is wonderful. Now you are finding out how it is to be making speeches here and speeches there. Not exactly a picnic, but a tremendous "growing" experience, and I know people love to listen to you, and not just for your

Yankee accent alone. You are a great girl, and people can learn a lot from just observing you.

Grandpa is going to Phoenix this weekend for a leadership meeting. The Church used to bring all the stake presidents from around the world to General Conference, but it got to be too much, so now they have leadership training for them in their area. Three hours on Friday night and four hours on Saturday. He will be home Saturday night and it is a good thing, because he is speaking in the Tabernacle Sunday night to all the institute students.

Laura is still looking for a summer job. It is not easy. Rosemary called me from the hospital this morning where she was waiting for Richard to get a cast on his broken elbow. He broke it playing basketball last night. Fortunately it is his left arm, as he will be going into finals in another week.

A letter from Celia yesterday said she had received the class schedule book from BYU but could hardly stand to look at it, as the thought of getting back into the real world was sickening. However, it is time for her to get home. She has worked her heart out and seems very tired. She has had some unbelievable experiences and has simply loved it. Seven more weeks to go and she is finishing up.

Grandma

Dear Jennie,

I am enclosing a story about your great, great, great, grandfather who lived in Liverpool, England. I concluded that since you are now in England and the English blood in you is beginning to stir, you should know something of your English background. Perhaps you can identify who William Minshall Evans is by remembering that he was Grandma Pay's grandfather. He was the father of Grandma Pay's mother. Is this as clear as mud? Well, no matter, just know that his blood flows in your veins.

We are all getting anxious to see Celia. She is leaving the mission with mixed feelings. She called her parents to see if it would be agreeable with them for her to extend another two weeks, but they had their trip all scheduled and set up to meet her on her release date of July 18 and could not accommodate her, which is just as well, as her release date is as providential as her call.

Just heard that Ebbie is going to Australia and another good friend to Hungary. Wow! What a church this is. We are going to Australia in November, but Australia is a big country, so who knows if we will see him.

But it would be great. Maybe he won't be there in November, as I don't know when he leaves.

Last Sunday we flew to St. Louis and visited with Heather and Tom and the two little boys. The next day we drove up to Nauvoo and Carthage and the Blairs followed us up in their car. Grandpa dedicated the new Carthage block on Tuesday and then we drove back to St. Louis to catch the flight home. They have restored Carthage Jail to the exact way it was when Joseph and Hyrum were murdered there 150 years ago. They acquired a whole city block surrounding the jail and have made it into a beautiful plaza with a marvelous statue of Joseph and Hyrum. Also added a fine visitor's center. It should become a great tourist attraction. Some 3,000 people were at the dedication, including President Benson.

We are so glad you are where you are, doing what you are doing. You are learning a lot and sometimes learning is painful, but it is also wonderful. Girls may come and go in that mission home, but there will never be a more delightful guest than our Jennie. Your letters are wonderful and give us a glimpse of some wonderful things that are happening to you as a person.

Love,

Grandma

Birthday Cards

The Hinckleys had 25 grandchildren, and Marjorie loved to send them birthday cards. This is just a small sampling of the kind of messages she included.

Dear Jennie,

We are so proud to be known as your grandparents. You are truly a beautiful and wonderful girl.

Much love,

Grandma and Grandpa Hinckley

✿

Dear Jennie,

This is the birthday you have been waiting for. May all your dreams come true. You are such a wonderful granddaughter I sometimes wonder if you are truly real. My challenge is to be worthy of you.

Grandpa joins me in sending you our love.

G. Hinckley

I am still thinking about the wonderful talk you gave in conference. You are such a terrific girl. You are gorgeous too!

Dear Jessica,

We hope you will always be the beautiful, wonderful good person that you are now. Grandpa and Grandma love you so much and are so proud of you. This is an important birthday as you will soon be baptized. You are so dear to us.

HAPPY BIRTHDAY!

Grandma & Grandpa Hinckley

❀

Dear Jessica,

Happy birthday! You get more beautiful inside and out every year. We feel such pride (righteous pride) and joy in you.

Lovingly,

Grandma & Grandpa Hinckley

Christmas Cards

The Hinckley grandchildren could count on receiving several Christmas cards each through-out the season. This helped build up the magic of the approaching holiday. A sleepover party with the children was another important event of the season.

Everything about Christmas is wonderful! Since it only comes once a year we will have to make it last forever in our hearts.

G & G Hinckley

Dear Jessica,

Look carefully at this picture. Is it the house where "Not a creature was stirring, not even a mouse?" Maybe except one little creature is stirring.

Merry Christmas!

Grandma Hinckley

Everything about Christmas is beautiful. XO

If we could only keep the spirit of Christmas every day of the year.

A granddaughter like you makes Christmas and every day a joy.
Hugs and kisses.
G & G Hinckley

✿

Love, Love, Love, Love

✿

Dear Mary,
Christmas is coming soon so be a good girl and please stay well! Can you come to the party on Dec. 23? Merry, Merry Christmas.

✿

Dear James,
I went with Jessica and Jonathan to the Christmas store in the Z.C.M.I. We saw this very funny Christmas card and thought you would like it.
Love,
Grandma Hinckley

✿

Invitation
Sunday, Dec. 18, 5:30
Christmas dinner and Fish pond.
Walk through Temple Square.

Thursday, Dec. 22, 7:00 p.m.

Christmas sleepover

A visit to Temple Square in the event we didn't make it Dec. 18

Friday, Dec. 23

Breakfast

2:00 p.m. "Annie" Promised Valley Playhouse

4:00 p.m. Straight home!

Love,

G. Hinckley

Postcards from Around the World

Sometimes Marjorie would arrive home from her travels before the postcards she sent had arrived, but it was still always a treat for her grandchildren to receive these mementoes of her travels.

Dear Celia,

We passed by this Ferris wheel in Vienna which is the highest Ferris wheel in the world.

Your Grandma and Grandpa Barnes stayed at the same hotel as we stayed at in Munich, so we spent a lot of time with them. It was such fun!

Love,

G & Gr Pa Hinckley

Dear girls,

Grandma Pay made herself a long red velvet skirt and she wears it with an old lace blouse that she wore when she was a little girl. She put it on and went off to see the ballet in a taxi the other night.

Aunt Joanne has a new baby girl. I haven't seen her yet. They named her Sarah Baird.

Love,

Grandma H.

This sunset is no exaggeration—when the sky is clear it is lovely—but it has rained a lot since we arrived.

Love

G.

We have about 3 leis like the ones in the picture, but I guess they will not last until we get home. They smell beautiful.

Love,

G.

The people here only dress in these costumes for special holidays and festivals, but we see many of them in the shops.

Love,

M

Dear Emily,

This is the way Jerusalem looks at night. It is such a beautiful city. We fell in love with it.

Love,

Grandma H.

Dear Rosie,

We spent two days in Vienna where Empress Elisabeth ruled for 61 years. She was greatly loved. The picture on Heidi's card shows one of the rooms in her palace. See you soon.

Love,

Grandma H.

✿

Dear little Laura,

There is a beautiful blue swimming pool just below our patio and when I see the children having fun in it I think of you and your new swimming suit.

Love,

M

✿

We now have a Mormon boy who is in the Queens Guard and has won all kinds of honors and is a popular fireside speaker in the London area.

Love,

M

✿

Dear James,

The Indians used to bring their beautiful princesses up to the top of this mountain so the warriors would not steal them away.

Maybe someday you will be a missionary and come to Peru. Who knows.

Love,

G. Hinckley

My dear little sweetheart Emily,

Thank you so much for your nice letter. I did not know that 4-year-olds could write letters. I am so proud of it that I have pasted it on my refrigerator door where I see it many times an hour. This is a picture of Cedar Breaks where we went with Clark. When we got there it was raining and hailing so hard we had to sit in the car while Clark went on a hike with his umbrella.

Love and kisses,

Grandma H.

Dear Amy,

The stake president gave me a large bouquet of yellow chrysanthemums and red roses when we got off the plane in Hong Kong. They are beautiful.

It was a long ride from San Francisco to Hong Kong—13½ hours. We flew all afternoon and all night.

Love,

Grandma Hinckley

This is a scene we see from our hotel window. There are many women washing clothes in the ocean and spreading them out on the rocks to dry, but they are not dressed as beautifully as the women in this picture. We are so happy to be in Korea again. Met with 40 missionaries this morning.

Love,

Grandma

Dear Rosemary,

I ordered a hamburger at McDonald's in Hong Kong and told them I wanted a plain bun without sesame seeds. They served me a plain bun with no hamburger, also just a little catsup. Our Chinese and their English is not all that good.

Hong Kong is more crowded than ever, but just as exciting as always.

Love,

G. Hinckley

Dear Rosie,

I am spending the afternoon alone in a fancy, new, modern hotel on the south coast of Korea. My hotel window looks down on the ocean with about 4 miles of beautiful sandy beach. It is a warm day and hundreds of people are out. I walked about 2 miles along the beach looking at the strange sights and smelling strange smells.

Love,

G. Hinckley

We have had a great time in Japan. We left early this morning and there were many there to see us off. 25–30 children came down to the airport and sang "I am a child of God" in Japanese. They gave us paper origami leis which they had made in Primary. We are now on the plane headed for Madrid. The stewardess is LDS. She is going to give us a lesson in origami. Weather is beautiful.

    Love,

    M

Dear little Emily,

    Yesterday we went deep sea fishing in a small boat which bounced and bounced on the waves. I thought it was very fun, but some people got seasick. Grandpa caught the first fish that was caught and it was a big one, but we had to give it away as we had no place to cook it.

    Love,

    M

Dear Heidi,

    They were selling strange things from little carts along the beach where I just returned from a walk. 3 little Korean girls had set up a box like a lemonade stand, but were selling big beautiful fresh strawberries in paper cups. They looked much better than the steaming, smelling fish in a big iron pot at the next stand.

    Love,

    Grandma Hinckley

Dear Laura,

We are in Pusan today with our friend Rhee Ho Nam. You have met him at our house at conference time. He went down to the beach at 6 a.m. this morning to get fresh shrimp from the first fishing boat that came in. We are eating it at his home tonight. It will be a real treat.

Love,

Grandma Hinckley

Dear Emily,

This is a typical street scene in Hong Kong. Grandpa and I had to hold onto each other so we wouldn't get separated and lost. The noise in the streets is so loud we have to shout to each other to be heard.

Love,

Grandma Hinckley

Dear Emily,

There are lots of people on the beach today but I have not seen one swim suit. The women are all in dresses, carrying their shoes in their hands and holding up their skirts while they wade out in the water. When the waves come up to their knees they scream and run back. It is hard to enjoy this alone. As I walked along the beach I pretended one of you was with me. Such strange sights.

Love,

Grandma Hinckley

Dear Rosemary,

There was a large group of people who met us at the airport in Pusan with many banners saying "Welcome Elder Hinckley." One banner said "Did you bring us a Stake?" In the middle of the crowd the Relief Society president made me stand still while she took my measurements for a Korean dress, as everyone looked on. Very embarrassing.

Love,

Grandma Hinckley

Dear Heather,

I never expect to be in a more beautiful spot. I hope someday you will see the harbor at Hilo. We had a meeting with the Saints here last night and the little Hawaiian children made me homesick for Heather. Be a good girl and don't forget us.

Love,

Grandma Hinckley

Our Angela,

Grandpa and I wandered into a park last night quite by accident where an outdoor orchestra was playing beautiful Strauss waltzes. There were floodlights on the Strauss monument shown in the upper right-hand corner of this card and it was all too lovely. We fell in love with Vienna.

Love,

G & Gr. Pa

Dear Katie,

Thank you for the nice letter you sent me. I am glad you had a Christmas tree. We had one too but it was an artificial tree. Not a real one. We have taken it down and put it away in the storage room. I am anxious to see the dolly Santa brought you. I love you very much.

Grandma Hinckley

✿

Dear Jeffie,

You would love to see all the animals in the streets of Jerusalem, camels and donkeys and sheep.

Love,

M

✿

Dear Heather,

Beethoven was born in Germany but lived most of his life in Vienna, Austria. We saw the houses where he lived marked with an X. We also saw where he went to sulfur springs to bathe his ears in the warm water when he began to go deaf, hoping he would prevent complete deafness. It was very impressive. He spent hours practicing every day in the house with the red flag. There was a woman who discovered what hours he practiced and would come each day and stand across the street to listen. When he learned about it he quit practicing there. We rested in Vienna Monday night and in the morning it was lovely.

See you soon.

Love,

G. & Grandpa H.

Afterword

In 1999, President Gordon B. Hinckley wrote the following tribute to his wife, Marjorie, to be included in the book Glimpses into the Life and Heart of Marjorie Pay Hinckley:

My darling,

It is now more than sixty years since we entered the Salt Lake Temple, there to be married for eternity. I had known you for a long time prior to that. I knew what I was getting into, and it has all turned out as I had hoped it would.

What a treasured companion you have been. Through all of these years we have walked side by side as equals before the Lord. There have been good days and bad days, but the good days have far outnumbered the bad ones.

Life for the most part has dealt gently with us. During the Depression, when we were newly married, we were poor and didn't know it because we were so rich in the things that really count. The laughter of happy children graced our kitchen table. The presence of a loving mother blessed our home. The Lord has opened the windows of heaven and showered down blessings too numerous to mention. He has smiled upon us in a wondrous way.

We have found comfort and gladness in one another and in our children. Now they have families of their own and grandchildren. All of our posterity have brought joy to our hearts.

When our children were young, you seldom traveled with me. I would be gone for as long as two months at a time. There were not even telephone calls permitted in those days. We wrote letters. You never complained. How wonderful it was to come home and be held warmly in your arms and those of our children.

Now in more recent years we have traveled far and wide together. We have visited every continent. We have held meetings in the great cities of the world and in many smaller ones. We have met the distinguished of the earth. We have spoken to millions who have appreciated you so greatly. With your familiar words you have won the love of all who have heard you. Your down-to-earth good sense, your sparkling and refreshing wit, your quiet and unfailing wisdom, and your tremendous and ever constant faith have won the hearts of all who have listened to you.

You have been my critic and my judge. You have seen to it that my shoes were shined, my suit pressed, my tie straight. You have pushed aside the flattery that comes with public life, and winnowed the kind and sincere words of honest and loving friends. You have held at bay that old fraud of adulation and kept my feet planted on the solid earth. How I appreciate you.

Your voracious appetite for reading and your relentless pursuit of knowledge have kept you alert and refreshing throughout a long and fruitful life.

Now we have grown old together, and it has been a sweet experience. We have shrunk in stature and move a little more slowly. We are more forgetful. But as of this writing we still have one another—and that is so good. And when in some future day the hand of death gently touches one or the other of us there will be tears, yes, but there will also be a quiet and certain assurance of reunion and eternal companionship.

"Trusty, dusky, vivid, true . . ."

The God of Heaven fashioned you.

I love you, dear,

Gordon

In his closing remarks in general conference in April 2004, President Hinckley made reference to an illness from which his wife had been suffering for several weeks:

"Some of you have noticed the absence of Sister Hinckley. For the first time in 46 years, since I became a General Authority, she has not attended general conference. Earlier this year, we were in Africa to dedicate the Accra Ghana Temple. On leaving there we flew to Sal, a barren island in the Atlantic, where we met with members of a local branch. We then flew to St. Thomas, an island in the Caribbean. There we met with a few others of our members. We were on our way home when she collapsed with weariness. She has had a difficult time ever since. She is now 92, a little younger than I am. I guess the clock is winding down, and we do not know how to rewind it."

Two days later, on Tuesday, April 6, Marjorie Pay Hinckley passed away. But she left a legacy of love and example and faith, and her letters as preserved here show only a tiny portion of what she gave the world. President Hinckley's remarks at Elder Neal A. Maxwell's funeral in July 2004, two months after her death, are a fitting epilogue to this collection:

"At funerals we speak words intended to give comfort. But in reality they afford but little comfort. Only those who have passed through this dark valley know its utter desolation. To lose one's much-loved partner with whom one has long walked through sunshine and shadow is absolutely devastating. There is a consuming loneliness which increases in intensity. It painfully gnaws at one's very soul. But in the quiet of the night a silent whisper is heard that says, 'All is well. All is well.' And that voice from out of the unknown brings peace, and certainty, and unwavering assurance that death is not the end, that life goes on, with work to do and victories to be gained. That voice quietly, even unheard with mortal ears, brings the assurance that, as surely as there has been separation, there will be a joyful reuniting.

"And so with that firm assurance you will go on. There will be days of loneliness and nights of longing, but the sunlight of faith will shine again and the fires of love will warm you."